A Methodology for Building the Data Lakehouse

Bill Inmon

Ranjeet Srivastava

Patty Haines

Technics Publications

115 Linda Vista, Sedona, Arizona, USA

https://www.TechnicsPub.com

Edited by Jamie Hoberman

Cover design by Lorena Molinari

First Printing 2024

ISBN, print ed.   9781634624183
ISBN, Kindle ed.   9781634624190
ISBN, PDF ed.   9781634624206

Acknowledgments

Most acknowledgments for a book refer to contributions made by fellow authors or other contributors. This acknowledgment is different. This acknowledgment is about an organization that has made no direct contribution. Instead, it is indirect because this book would not exist without their contribution.

Last year, Porter Hospital Transplant Center in Denver gave me a kidney transplant. Without their extreme competence, this book would not exist. The level of care and the competency of the doctors could not have been better throughout the journey. I compliment and thank Porter for their wonderful care. In particular, I thank:

- Dr Alexander Wiseman
- Dr Alan Hawxby
- Dr Thomas Collins
- Dr Mauricio Orrego
- Dr Karl Womer
- Dr Scott Davis
- Dr Hunter Moore
- Buffy Cass
- Holly Ebach
- Liz Poste
- Liz Poste

- Vanessa Jamison
- Sarah Brantley
- Diane Thompson
- Michelle Dotson
- Kellie Ryan
- Brenna Crosby
- Jacinto Gosbeth
- Amy Kearns
- Karlie Wipperling
- Alison Burnett
- Kat Denton
- Melissa Rogers
- Megan Pitts
- Jessica Coleman
- Michelle Gergis
- Samantha Carillo
- Cassandra Akins-Buckingham
- Danielle Vogt
- Kat Denton
- Jennifer Lurie
- Adrianne Rodriguez
- Hannah Cerf
- In intensive care – Sam Ortiz

In addition, I thank my family physician, Dr Chad Boekes. And a final special thanks to Alexis Beuhler, whose care, competency, and kindness were simply the best.

Bill Inmon

Contents

CHAPTER 1

Overview

Let's start with what data goes into the data lakehouse. The different kinds of data that go into the data lakehouse shape its structure, contents, and usage. Structured, textual, and analog/IoT data form the basis for the modern data lakehouse. There are other types of data in the organization, but these three categories encompass the vast majority of the data found in the organization.

Corporate data

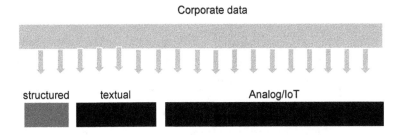

structured   textual   Analog/IoT

Figure 1-1. The different kinds of data in the data lakehouse.

Architecture and technology

There is a difference between architecture and technology. Consider the building of a bridge. The architect of the bridge considers:

- How much traffic will pass over the bridge?
- What kind of traffic will pass over the bridge?
- How will the materials of the bridge age?
- What forces of nature must the bridge withstand?
- Will boats need to pass beneath the bridge?

The technician building the bridge considers:

- Where will this nail go?
- Where are my concrete forms?
- Where do I place the reinforcing rods?
- Where is the limber that I need?

Both the architect and the technician are needed. Both have legitimate concerns. But the concerns and issues that they face are very different.

Complicating matters is that the data lakehouse architecture and the platform it resides on are independent. You can build a data lakehouse on a variety of platforms. Some platforms are better than others, but there is no connection between a platform and the architecture of the data lakehouse. Indeed, if desired, you can build the data lakehouse over more than one platform at the same time.

The data lakehouse is a complex architecture. There are many different parts to the architecture. Furthermore, you can follow many different paths in constructing the data lakehouse. There is no such thing as a "right" path. There are many "right" paths in the building of the data lakehouse.

For the original description of the data lakehouse architecture, please refer to the books:

- *Rise of the Data Lakehouse*, by Bill Inmon and Ranjeet Srivastava.
- *The Data Lakehouse: The Bedrock for Artificial Intelligence, Machine Learning, and Data Mesh*, by Bill Inmon, Dave Rapien, and Valerie Bartelt.
- *The Data Lakehouse Architecture*, by Bill Inmon and Ranjeet Srivastava.

Starting with the data lake

Most organizations start their journey to the data lakehouse by building a data lake. In a data lake, raw data is thrown into the data lake in the hopes that it will be useful for analytical processing. And in short order, the data lake turns into a data swamp and:

- Is expensive
- Serves no useful purpose
- Is getting worse each day.

At this point, the organization decides to turn the data lake into a data lakehouse. Even though they sound similar and have similar characteristics, the data lake and the data lakehouse are architecturally very different. But not everyone starts with the swamp that is the data lake. Some people start with applications, some with the vestiges of an earlier data warehouse, and some with a combination.

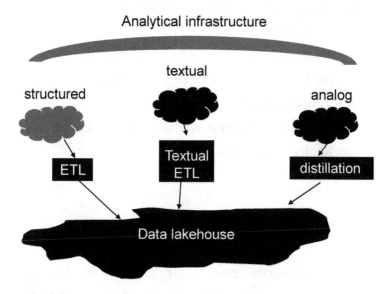

Figure 1-2. The essential ingredients of the data lakehouse are an analytical infrastructure, the raw data vetted and transformed before being loaded into the data lakehouse, and the data lakehouse itself.

The primary objective of the data lakehouse is to support analytical processing. Although the data in the data lakehouse can support operational processing, operational transaction processing occurs outside the data lakehouse.

Each data lakehouse component plays an important role in building and using the data lakehouse.

The analytical infrastructure

The analytical infrastructure sits over the data lakehouse and contains the metadata needed to find the desired data.

The primary purpose of the analytical infrastructure is to allow the analyst to find and understand the data found in the data lakehouse. The analytical infrastructure points to the data in the data lakehouse.

The analytical infrastructure contains many different components. Each of the different kinds of data in the data lakehouse requires its own form of metadata. And the forms of metadata are indeed very different. In addition, the analytical infrastructure allows the different types of metadata to be related to each other, if indeed, there is a relationship in the real world.

Although building the analytical infrastructure takes effort, the analytical infrastructure needs to be constantly updated and maintained. There are several reasons for the constant changing of the analytical infrastructure:

- The data lakehouse is constantly changing.
- Business conditions reflected by the data lakehouse are constantly changing.
- The end user is constantly changing his/her mind about what data needs to be analyzed and how that data needs to be analyzed.

For these reasons and more, the analytical infrastructure is in constant motion.

Raw data and transformation

The second component of the data lakehouse is the raw data that needs to be vetted and transformed before being placed in the data lakehouse.

The primary purpose of vetting raw data before it arrives in the data lakehouse is to prepare it for analytical processing.

Note that placing raw data in the data lakehouse without transformation does no good. Each of the different kinds of data requires its own unique form of transformation. Structured data passes through standard Extract, Transform, and Load (ETL) processing. Textual data passes through textual ETL. Analog/IoT data passes through a distillation process.

Structured ETL is very different from textual ETL. Textual ETL is very different from distillation. And distillation is very different from structured ETL processing. There is little or no similarity of the transformation processes with each other.

There are multiple paths to the building of the data lakehouse. There is no such thing as a "right" path. The three common paths are:

- Building the structured component of the data lakehouse
- Building the textual component of the data lakehouse
- Building the analog/IoT component of the data lakehouse.

There is no prescribed order to build these components. Some of the approaches to building are:

- Build the structured component, the textual component, and then the analog component
- Build only the structured component
- Build the structured component and the textual component
- Build the analog component, the structured component, and then the textual component.

The order is determined by the type of data and the need for analytical processing against that data. On the other hand, once we choose the individual type of data, there is a prescribed order for transforming the type of data. Furthermore, it is perfectly normal and acceptable to load different types of data into the data lakehouse simultaneously. One organization loads data into the data lakehouse at the same time as another organization is loads other types of data into the data lakehouse, and this simultaneous loading of data is very normal and acceptable.

There are, of course, synchronization issues and resource issues to address during the simultaneous loading of data. But it is absolutely normal to load multiple types of data into the data lakehouse at the same time.

The rate of growth of the data lakehouse

Another perspective of the building of the data lakehouse is the rate at which the data lakehouse grows. We never load the data lakehouse all at once. Instead, we load iteratively. On day one, some data is loaded into the data lakehouse. On day two, more data is loaded. On day three, more data is loaded, and so forth.

Day 1   Day 2   Day 3   Day 4   Day 5

Figure 1-3. The data lakehouse is built gradually over time.

Trying to build the data lakehouse all at once is a serious mistake.

CHAPTER 2

The Structured Environment and the Data Lakehouse

The structured environment consists of row after row of data that is structured the same. Although the structure of the data is the same, the contents of the structured records are not. For example, customer ABC walks into Walmart and purchases milk. A record is made of customer ABC's purchase. Now, customer BCD purchases bread at Walmart. Walmart makes a record of that purchase. The records of the two purchases have an identical format and structure. But the contents of the records are different. One record is for customer ABC's milk and the other record is for customer BCD's bread.

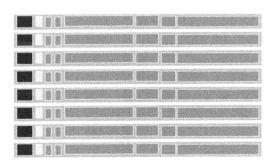

Figure 2-1. Each record is different, but the structure of each record is the same.

Structured components

The structured environment contains these components:

- Keys – identifying information for the record
- Attributes – further information about the record
- Indexes – the codified information about the location of a record

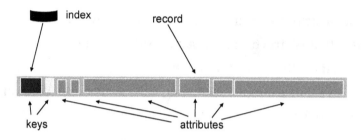

Figure 2-2. The components of structured data.

Transactions

The source of transactions is the record of the execution of some activity, such as:

- Bank deposits
- Phone calls
- Payments
- Reservations in an airline.

The transaction enters the computer, accesses data, is transacted against the data, and is recorded in the database. The application is the computer software that governs the activity of the computer and the proper conduct of the transaction.

Different perspectives

Applications run much of the business of organizations. We build applications for the specific requirements of some organization within the organization. Almost always, the applications apply to the needs of a specific department. Therefore, there are many different applications spread across the organization.

The problem with an organization having lots of applications is that the organization cannot achieve an enterprise view of what is going on with the entire organization. Yet, organizations need this enterprise perspective to make informed decisions. To this end, there is a need for both application and enterprise-wide data. Application differs from enterprise data in several ways, including:

- Names of data elements are different
- Data is encoded differently
- Measurements are made in different denominators
- Time is calculated differently
- Amounts of money have different currency exchange rates.

There are many ways in which application designers shape their data, and for the business analyst to look across the organization and achieve an enterprise view of data, the business analyst needs to normalize the data into a consistent definition and format. As a simple example of the need for normalizing data into a corporate format and structure, different applications have encoded gender differently. There needs to be a single enterprise way of understanding gender.

Application data needs to be converted into enterprise data.

Data modeling

The data model is the guiding light for transforming application data into enterprise data. The data model describes what the enterprise data needs to look like at an abstract level. Once the data model is in place, the designer can start to understand the needed transformations. The designer starts with application data. The designer then determines what to do to the application data to transform it into enterprise data.

Transformation is designed by understanding the input, understanding the output, and then specifying how the input gets to be in the form and format of the output.

How is the data model built?

There are actually many ways of building a data model. Let's cover the classical method of designing a data model.

We start by interviewing the end user groups that are stakeholders in the system to learn their business processes and data needs. The descriptions gathered from interviews help determine the data elements that interest the end users.

After the raw data elements that are needed are collected, the designer then takes that raw data elements and determines which data elements are:

- Extraneous?
- Summarized?
- Derived?

These kinds of data need to be removed from the data model because they constantly change and require documenting the logic used to produce them. They are added back into the system when performing actual analytics. After removing the summarized and derived data, we organize the data elements into logical groupings. The notion of existence criteria determines the logical groupings. For example, a customer's address does not exist until there is a customer. A part number description does not exist unless there is first a part. A store location does not exist unless there is first a store.

Data model

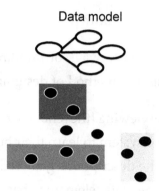

Figure 2-3. The data that is dependent on something is grouped according to its dependency. We call this process the "normalization" of data.

For example, a customer has a name, address, gender, and so forth. A part has a part number, a description, a unit of measure, and so forth. A store has a location, a manager, a telephone number, and so forth. After the groups of data elements are collected, edited, and grouped, the next step is to define the key values for the group.

Data model

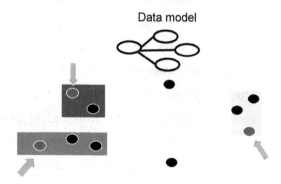

Figure 2-4. The key value determines how the computer system will locate the grouping of data. As a rule, the key value is unique. But occasionally, the key will include non-unique data as well.

Non-unique keys are specified when the data needs to be accessed by key value. For example, we may specify gender by key. In doing so, the end user analyst can easily access all of the women or all of the men in the database.

As an example of key identification, a human may have an identifying Social Security Number. Or a telephone will have its unique number. Or a store will have its name and its address. The groupings of data can now be located by the computer using the defined key values.

After the keys of the groupings of data are defined, the next step is to identify the relationships among the different groupings. For example, a customer may buy a product. So, we create a link between customer and product. Or a manufacturer may produce a product. We create a link between manufacturer and product.

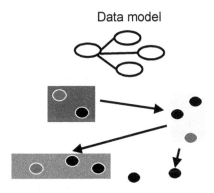

Figure 2-5. We identify the relationships between the elements.

At this point, the designer is prepared to create the data model. The general groupings of data become the entities or major subject areas of the organization.

Each of the major entities of the organization has a lower-level definition. The lower-level definition is the data item set (dis). Each entity has a dis, which contains the keys and the non-key attributes that belong to this entity.

After the dis is created, the dis is further amplified by adding physical specifications to the keys and attributes found in the dis. These specifications, called Data Definition Language (DDL), define the data to the database.

Different levels

The general structure of the data model looks like the different kinds of world maps. The globe represents the earth at the highest level, where Europe and Africa are clearly delineated. Then there is Texas, which is merely a small spot on the globe. Then, inside Texas is Dallas. Dallas is just another city in Texas.

The highest level of the data model is usually referred to as the Entity Relationship Diagram (ERD).

Each level of mapping describes a different aspect of the earth. You would not use a map of Dallas to describe Asia. And you would not use a globe to describe how to get from Johannesburg to Cape Town. Similarly, you would not use the ERD level of the data model to describe the key structure of a part number. Nor would you use the DDL description of the part number to show how customers relate to their birthplace.

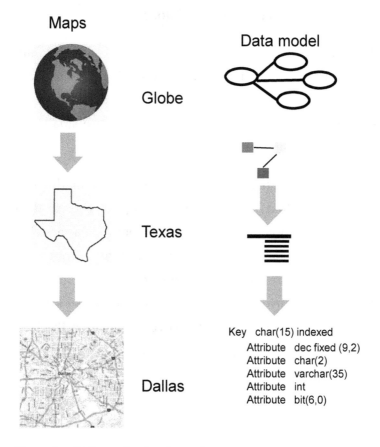

Figure 2-6. Different levels of mapping.

Constant change

While building the data model is elaborate and complex, even when built properly, the data model is constantly changing due to:

- Changing business requirements
- Changing legislation
- More competition
- Changing economic conditions.

The good news is that usually these changes are incremental and small. Whole sections of the data model rarely have to be discarded and recast. Under nearly every circumstance, the changes made over time are small and almost incidental.

While most organizations build their own data model, it is worth noting that there are such things as generic data models. The whole notion behind a generic data model is that there is a great deal of similarity from one organization to another within the same industry. Therefore, acquiring an industrial data model can save an enormous amount of time. However, even with the best generic data model, a certain amount of customization is needed.

Once the model is ready

While there is no question that getting the data model is a huge step forward, what happens after the data model is ready to go?

Once the data model is built, the next step is to formally define your enterprise data.

In many ways, the data model is the starting point for the design of enterprise data. But the data model is only part of the story. The definition of the corporate data needs to include such things as:

- Encodings
- Calculation
- Measurements.

After the corporate data definition is done, the next step is to prioritize which applications will be processed and the order in which they will be processed. There are many different criteria for the prioritization of the applications. Some of the factors for prioritization include:

- Which application is the closest to the heart of the business?
- Which application has the largest business impact?
- Which application is the most critical?
- Which application is the largest?
- Which application is oldest?

After all the factors are considered, the applications that will be vetted first are determined. We create a prioritization list.

The needed input to enterprise data is used to determine what data the first application will supply. Next, we select the data from the first application and compare it to the structure in the data model, which yields the necessary transformations. Then, the next data element from the first application is considered and treated in the same way. This process continues until all the data needed from the first application is processed.

Transformations

For example, consider application gender is designated a m,f. In the enterprise data, gender is represented as male, female. So if input value is F, the output value is Female. As another example, if the input value is measured in inches, the output value is measured in inches divided by twelve, which yields the same value in feet. Note that it is normal to have much more complex transformations than these two simple examples.

In addition, the first example is an example of encoding transformation. The second example is an example of measurement normalization. Many more types of transformation occur as application data is transformed into corporate data.

After the transformation process is defined, the next step is to place the transformation into the ETL process. Then, the data is actually read in the input file by ETL, processed by ETL, and the output data is loaded into the enterprise data file.

After the first application file is processed, the next step is to repeat the process for the next application in the prioritized queue. Finally, all the data to load into the enterprise data file is loaded into the file. Of course, when the data is loaded into the enterprise data file, it becomes enterprise data, not application data.

Change over time

Given the size and complexity of the steps and that the business is constantly changing, realize that change is inevitable in building enterprise data. The good news is that, normally, change is incremental. Only on catastrophic occasions does a whole portion of corporate data need to be reworked.

In addition, it needs to be recognized that change can occur anywhere in the process. Change can be in the data model. Change can be in the rules of transformation.

Change can occur in the originating applications themselves. And change can occur in the corporate data itself.

When the enterprise data file is sufficiently populated, the enterprise data file can be loaded into the data lakehouse.

CHAPTER 3

Text and the Data Lakehouse

There is great business value wrapped up in text. Examples include:

- Customer sentiment
- Medical record research
- Contract analysis
- Insurance claims processing

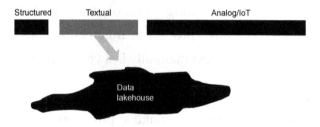

Figure 3-1. Textual data is an important part of the data lakehouse.

Challenges with text

But data that is wrapped up in the form of text presents great challenges to the organization. And that is a shame because the value of data wrapped up in text is larger than that found anywhere else in the organization.

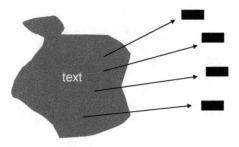

Figure 3-2. **As long as important information is wrapped up in the form of text, it is difficult to analyze.**

The large volume of text presents the biggest challenge for generating business value because text must be read manually to be understood. It is time-consuming and inefficient to read huge amounts of text manually. Furthermore, even the best minds have limited capacity. This means that reading lots of textual documents manually is very error-prone. For this reason alone, trying to read and analyze text manually is a very bad idea.

But dealing with volumes of text is not the only challenge in using text for decision-making purposes. The second challenge in reading and analyzing text is the need for disambiguation. To understand the meaning of text, we must also understand its context. And context is not obvious and can be very complex. For example, when someone says, "I fired the gun," the person pulled the trigger of a loaded gun. Or if the person says, "My boss fired me," the person means they lost their job. Although the same word "fire" was used, it has two very different meanings.

For the volumes of text to be read and analyzed, it is necessary to enlist the aid of the computer. But to enlist the aid of the computer, we must overcome some challenges. Simply putting text into a computer does little good. Instead, the computer has to understand:

- What words are important and what words are not important
- The context of those words
- The order and sequencing of those words.

Furthermore, the computer needs to understand that there are a lot of words that are only necessary for proper speech but do not greatly impact what is being said. These words need to be discarded for efficient and incisive processing against text. These extraneous words merely get in the way of analytical processing.

Ingesting text

The first of these challenges is the simple act of ingesting the text. Text comes in many forms and over many different media. For the computer to be able to read and analyze text, the text must first be captured and reduced to a form compatible with the computer. Some of the typical places to find text are:

- Print
- Voice

- Internet
- Spreadsheet
- Email.

It turns out that each of these sources of text has their own issues and idiosyncrasies.

Ingesting print

One of the oldest and, in some ways, the most pervasive source of text is print. Print occurs in newspapers, magazines, corporate reports, letters, and in many other places.

Optical Character Recognition (OCR) technology reads and converts print to an electronic format. OCR technology is not new. It has been in existence for quite a while. On the whole, OCR technology is quite reliable and accurate. However, some issues can greatly affect the quality of OCR's print-to-electronic transcription.

OCR works well as long as the font is of a standard type. But there are many different font types, and OCR does not receive some of them well. A second issue affecting the quality of OCR processing is that of ink strike. If the ink strike is too faint, OCR has difficulty reading the text. A third issue affecting the quality of the output of OCR is that of the paper quality on which the text is printed. If the paper is old and brittle, the submission of the paper to OCR processing can destroy the paper itself.

Ingesting voice

The second media that text arrives in is in the form of voice. Voice is the oldest form of text. Voice arrives in the organization through call centers, meetings, telephone conversations, and so forth.

Voice is recorded and fed into voice transcription technology. Voice transcription technology then listens to the recording and turns the recording into electronic text.

Instead of doing voice transcription manually, which is prohibitively expensive, you can use automated voice transcription, such as Nuance, Zoom, Google, or Microsoft.

However, the problem with voice transcription is that it is never 100% accurate. Inevitably, some words are misunderstood and arrive in the transcription incorrectly. Factors that affect the quality of the transcription include the quality of the recording itself, the person's accent, and the force of the person's voice (some people speak loudly whereas others speak softly).

Ingesting from the internet

One of the best sources of text is the Internet. There is a wide diversity of text on the Internet. And there are no privacy concerns for data found on the Internet.

However, there are drawbacks to using the Internet as a source for text. The first drawback is that some sites do not want you reading and analyzing their data. These sites go out of their way to make capturing data difficult. Another challenge is that each site is different. This means that the interface to capture data must be custom-written for each site. And to add to the challenge, the sites change often, making for the constant maintenance of custom programs. Yet another challenge is that some sites attract bogus comments. Bots write some of the comments on the site.

Ingesting text from spreadsheets

Next to print, the most ubiquitous form of text resides in spreadsheets. The good news is that spreadsheets already have the data in an electronic format. The challenge with text then becomes:

- Lifting the text off of the spreadsheet
- Understanding the meaning of the text
- Believing the text that has been lifted.

As an example of the unbelievability of spreadsheet data, I can create a spreadsheet that says that Bill Inmon makes $1,000,000 a month. The spreadsheet says that, but it is not true.

Another issue with spreadsheets is that, under normal circumstances, we cannot lift numeric values from a spreadsheet. The reason is that there is no metadata description of the numeric data. The problem is that there is no reliable metadata on the spreadsheet that clearly defines the meaning of the numeric value.

Ingesting email

Another good source of textual information is email. Emails can contain valuable information from customers and business associates. Text is already in the form of electronic text when found in an email.

However, there are several other issues associated with reading and interpreting email. The first issue is that email contains a lot of spam and blather. We must eliminate the spam and blather before the email stream becomes meaningful. In addition, email carries a significant amount of system overhead we must remove before the email can be efficiently processed.

Ingestion

We must convert text to a form of electronic text before it becomes useful for text analysis. This process of converting and editing text is called the "ingestion" process and is essential to reading and analyzing text.

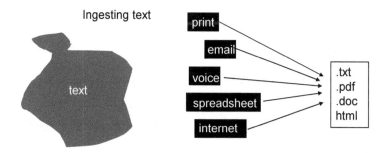

Figure 3-3. Putting text into an electronic text format.

Other issues

However, there are other issues relating to the reading and analysis of text other than ingestion, including:

- Text can come in the form of many languages
- Text can be slang
- Text can be misspelled
- Text can take on different meanings when it is in proximity to other text
- Text can be intermixed with structured data
- Text is often full of acronyms, which need to be understood accurately.

Context

In a word, understanding text and making the proper interpretation of the meaning of text is a complex issue. The key to being able to read and analyze text is to have both text and context as part of the equation.

The taxonomy

There are many facets to capturing and understanding the context of text. The most important tool in the capture of the context of text is a taxonomy. Taxonomies are needed to start reading and analyzing text.

> *A simple definition of a taxonomy is that the taxonomy is the classification of like elements of data.*

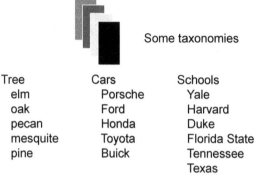

Some taxonomies

Tree	Cars	Schools
elm	Porsche	Yale
oak	Ford	Harvard
pecan	Honda	Duke
mesquite	Toyota	Florida State
pine	Buick	Tennessee
		Texas

Figure 3-4. A tree may be an elm, oak, or pecan tree. A car may be a Porsche, Honda, or a Toyota. A college might be Yale, Harvard, or Princeton.

Taxonomies can encompass a wide variety of topics. In fact, there are an almost infinite number of taxonomies. The analyst chooses the taxonomies that are relevant to their project. What is not a taxonomy is just a common list of words. For example, if the list included Porsche, Ford, and Honda, and also enchiladas, Cornell, and filet mignon, the list would not be a taxonomy.

The ontology

Taxonomies are combined to form an ontology.

> *An ontology is a collection of taxonomies.*

Every business has many facets: customers, products, sales, advertising, employees, etc. A collection of taxonomies taken together is needed to reflect the business's different facets. As an example of an ontology, consider the example of a geographical collection of taxonomies. There is a taxonomy for countries of the world. There is a taxonomy for the states of a country. There is a taxonomy for the cities of the country. Each of the taxonomies can exist independently. Yet, there still is a relationship between the different taxonomies. These taxonomies form an ontology.

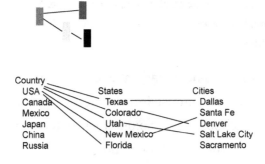

Country		
USA	States	Cities
Canada	Texas	Dallas
Mexico	Colorado	Santa Fe
Japan	Utah	Denver
China	New Mexico	Salt Lake City
Russia	Florida	Sacramento

Figure 3-5. An ontology example.

There are three levels to an ontology:

- **The generic level**. The generic level reflects language that is used generically, such as expressions of sentiment. Expressions of sentiment are for anything. You can like a car. You can like a steak. You can like a beach. The Internet is a good source of generic words and phrases.

- **The industrial level**. An industrial word is a word that is peculiar to a given industry. There are medical terms. There are legal terms. There are accounting terms, and so forth. These terms that have specific meanings inside the industry form this portion of the ontology. The best source for the industrial terms is Wand Technology. Wand has the world's largest collection of industrial terms and words.

- **The specific level**. The specific term is a term that only has meaning in the context of the organization being analyzed. For example, the term "CA098172-jp" may have meaning inside a particular oil company, but nowhere else. Specific terms must be captured individually from the documents of the organization.

All three types of terms must be part of an ontology to analyze text. Constructing one's own set of terms and words is always possible for an ontology. But it is strongly advised that this is not a good path to follow. It is much less expensive and much more efficient to use ontologies that already exist.

Acronyms

Another part of text analytics that must be accounted for by the analyst is that of reading and understanding acronyms. Acronyms are used on a daily basis. But two professions make liberal use of acronyms – the medical profession and the military.

Word proximity

Another consideration in the disambiguation of text is the fact that on occasion certain words taken together have different meanings when separated. For example, when you hear the term "…Dallas cowboy" you think of a once great football team. But when you hear the terns separately, you think of a city in Texas and a man wearing a hat riding a horse and tending cattle. The analyst must know when words that are in proximity to each other have special meaning.

Inline contextualization

As important as taxonomies and ontologies are, they are not the only language constructs that the text analyst must consider. There is another whole class of language constructs, called inline contextualization, that must be understood in order for the text to be analyzed properly.

Inline contextualization encompasses a lot of language and textual conventions. For example, if there are three digits followed by another three digits followed by four digits. It can be inferred that the digits represent a telephone number in the United States. Or names can be commonly recognized by looking for John, Mary, Susan, and Willam, for example.

Textual ETL

With textual ETL you:

- Select the taxonomies you need to use and combine them into an ontology
- Customize the ontology, if necessary
- Ingest the text
- Feed into textual ETL.

The output is a standard database that can be used for text analytics.

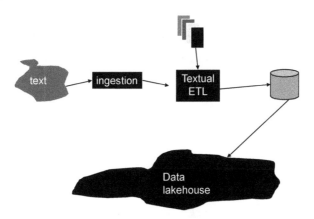

Figure 3-6. Once the database is created, it is ready to be placed in the data lakehouse.

CHAPTER 4

Analog Data and the Data Lakehouse

The data lakehouse consists of three types of data: structured, textual, and analog/IoT data. This discussion is on analog data. Although most organizations have some form of analog data, it is possible that they do not have any useful analog data.

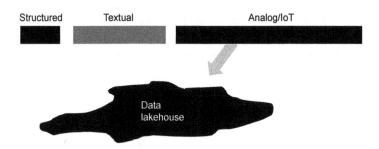

Figure 4-1. An important component of the data lakehouse is analog/IoT data.

Analog data is data that is generated by the operation of a machine. Stated differently, analog data is machine-generated data. The machine is in operation. The machine generates measurements as to how the machine is running and what the output of the machine is. Data is created by the operation of many different machines. Surveillance cameras take snapshots at intervals. Temperature gauges measure the temperature of a process. Drones spin around in the sky gathering information. Wristwatches generate their own information. And many more types of mechanical devices generate data as a normal part of their operation.

Machine-generated data plays an important role in some places, such as a manufacturing environment, where machines examine and measure the manufacturer's output. In other environments, machines only play an incidental role.

The vast majority of analog data has little or no business value. But a small part of analog data has great value.

To understand this perspective of analog data, consider the work done by a surveillance camera. When the surveillance camera looks over a parking lot at night, it sees an empty lot. Then, when the surveillance camera is on at 8:00 am, it sees cars arriving and being parked. Around 5:00 pm, the surveillance camera sees people going to their cars and driving off. On weekends, the parking lot contains very few cars. In truth, the day-to-day activities examined by the surveillance camera are boring and have little or no business value. However, one day there is an accident in the parking lot. One car has driven into another car causing damage. The 15 seconds captured by the surveillance camera that describe the accident suddenly become very important. From a percentage perspective, the data found in the surveillance camera is not useful most of the time. Occasionally, however, the images the surveillance camera finds are worth their weight in gold.

The implications of this disparity of data is that we need to separate data needs into two categories upon leaving the mechanical device. Most of the unuseful data needs to be sent to one place, and the useful data needs to be sent to the data lakehouse.

Figure 4-2. Some unuseful data has no business value and should be trashed. But if there is a chance that the unuseful data may contain something that might be useful in the future, then the unuseful data needs to be stored in some form of bulk storage.

Machine-generated data

Machine-generated data can be from sensors, instruments, etc. Human-generated data can be from emails, files, images, video, audio, social media etc. Business-generated data can be from agreements, contracts, invoices, presentations, legal or technical documents, etc. In the case of analog data, we will be primarily talking about machine-generated analog data. For example, when you take a picture with your phone's camera, your phone automatically generates machine data surrounding the image, such as the image's timestamp, host device name, pixel dimensions, image size, camera focal length, aperture, ISO, and other metadata.

As one of the largest contributors to the data lakehouse, machine data is extremely useful because it provides a complete, up-to-date status of everything, from user activity and transactional data to applications, servers, and networks. After all, the number of datasets generated and collected is increasing yearly, fueled by increased technologies and the Internet of Things (IoT). Remember, though, that all of this generated data might not be of direct use for analytics.

The more companies incorporate machine data into their analytics, the more equipped they'll be to make better business decisions.

As we learned so far, analog data in data analytics refers to continuous, real-world data represented as a continuous range of values. This type of data is often collected through sensors, instruments, or measurements and can take on any value within a specified range. Analog data is inherently continuous and can include measurements like temperature, pressure, voltage, or analog audio signals.

We also learned about a special characteristic of analog data: a tiny portion of the analog data might be important and a large portion might not.

In contrast to digital data, which is discrete and represented in binary form (0s and 1s), analog data is continuous and can have infinite possible values within its range. Analyzing analog data often involves techniques such as signal processing, statistical analysis, and visualization to extract meaningful insights and patterns.

In the context of machine learning and data modeling, analog data may need to be preprocessed or transformed into a suitable format for analysis. This could involve techniques like feature scaling, smoothing, or resampling to prepare the data for training machine learning models.

Understanding the nature of your data, whether it's analog or digital, is crucial when working on data analytics and machine learning projects, as it can impact the choice of algorithms and preprocessing steps you need to apply.

As mentioned, analog data may need to be preprocessed or transformed into a suitable format for analysis. So, we must learn more about the preprocessing part of analog data so that it is ready to be analyzed and consumable by your machine learning algorithms. After its transformation, you may use the data to train your machine learning models.

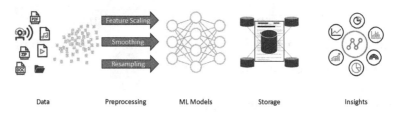

| Data | Preprocessing | ML Models | Storage | Insights |

Figure 4-3. Data preprocessing and readiness.

We can use techniques like feature scaling, smoothing, and resampling to prepare analog data.

Feature scaling

Feature scaling is a preprocessing technique used in data analytics and machine learning to standardize or normalize the range of features or variables in your dataset, including analog data. It ensures that all features have a similar scale, which can be important for certain machine learning algorithms and models. Feature scaling does not change the underlying distribution of the data; it only scales the values to a common range.

When working with analog data or any continuous data, you may encounter features with different units, scales, or ranges. Feature scaling helps in the following ways:

- **Equalizes the impact**: Some machine learning algorithms, like gradient descent-based optimization, can converge faster when features are on a similar scale. If one feature has values in the thousands while another has values in the tens, the algorithm might give more weight to the former, which can lead to suboptimal results.

- **Improves model interpretability**: Scaling ensures that coefficients or weights assigned to features in linear models are directly comparable. This makes it easier to interpret the importance of each feature in the model.

Two common methods for feature scaling are min-max scaling (normalization) and z-score scaling (standardization). Min-max scaling (normalization) scales the data to a specific range, often between 0 and 1. There is a standard statistical formula for min-max scaling that helps calculate the scaled value by deducting the minimum value of the feature from the original feature value, divided by the sum of the feature's maximum value minus the feature's minimum value. It can be represented as:

```
Xsc=(X - Xmin)/(Xmax - Xmin)
```

Where X is the original feature value, Xsc is the scaled value, Xmax is the maximum value of the feature, and Xmin is the minimum value of the feature.

Min-max normalization is a simple technique that rescales the data values to a range between 0 and 1, using the minimum and maximum values of the original data. This technique preserves the relative order and distance of the data points but also reduces the variance and magnifies the effect of outliers. Min-max normalization is useful when the data has a fixed range, such as grades or percentages, but it can distort the data if there are extreme values or different scales.

For a dataset, for example, we could guesstimate the min and max observable values as 30 and −10. We can then normalize any value, like 16.8, as follows:

```
Xsc = (X - Xmin) / (Xmax - Xmin)
Xsc = (16.8 - (-10)) / (30 -
(-10))
Xsc = 26.8 / 40
Xsc = 0.67
```

And you can see the range of the scaled value (or rescaled value) here, is between 0 and 1 only.

You might have noticed that if an X value (in the above example, it is 16.8) is outside the bounds of the minimum and maximum values (that is 30 and −10 as given above), the resulting value will not be in the range of 0 and 1. You could check for these observations before making predictions and remove them from the dataset or limit them to the pre-defined maximum or minimum values.

Z-score scaling (standardization) scales the data to have a mean (average) of 0 and a standard deviation of 1. A standard statistical formula for Z-score scaling also helps calculate the scaled value by dividing the difference between the original feature value and the mean of the feature by the standard deviation of the feature.

It can be represented as:

$$Xsc = (X - \mu) / \sigma$$

Where X is the original feature value, Xsc is the scaled value, μ is the mean of the feature, and σ is the standard deviation of the feature. For example, suppose we have the following data set:

Analog data
3
5
5
8
9
12
12
13
15
16
17
19
22
24
25
134

Through standard statistical calculations, we can find that the mean of the dataset is 21.2 and the standard deviation is 29.8. To perform a Z-score standardization on the first value in the dataset, we can use the following formula:

```
Xsc = (X - μ) / σ
Xsc = (3 - 21.2) / 29.8
Xsc = -0.61 (the new value)
```

You can use this formula to perform a Z-score standardization on every value in the dataset:

Analog data	Z-score value
3	-0.61
5	-0.54
5	-0.54
8	-0.44
9	-0.41
12	-0.31
12	-0.31
13	-0.28
15	-0.21
16	-0.17
17	-0.14
19	-0.07
22	0.03
24	0.09
25	0.13
134	3.79

The mean of the normalized values is 0 and the standard deviation of the normalized values is 1. The last value in the dataset is 3.79 standard deviations above the mean.

The benefit of performing this type of standardization is that the clear outlier in the dataset (134) has been transformed in such a way that it's no longer a massive outlier. If we then use this dataset to fit some type of machine learning model, the outlier will no longer have as big of an influence as it might have on the model fit.

Ultimately, the choice of scaling method depends on the nature of your data and the requirements of your machine learning model. Min-max scaling is suitable when you must preserve the original data's distribution and know the minimum and maximum values are meaningful. Standardization is often preferred when dealing with models that assume a standard normal distribution of features, such as many clustering algorithms.

Before applying feature scaling, splitting your data into training and testing sets is essential to avoid data leakage. Additionally, feature scaling should be applied separately to training and testing sets, using the statistics (min, max, mean, and standard deviation) computed from the training set to ensure consistency.

There are a few other normalization techniques as well, like decimal scaling normalization, log transformation normalization, etc.

So, when should we think of normalize or standardize our analog data?

The answer is simple. Since these are preprocessing techniques, whether your input variables require scaling depends on the specifics of your problem and the solutions you need for your analytics purpose. For example, you may have a sequence of quantities as inputs, such as prices or temperatures.

So, if the distribution of the quantity is normal, then it should be standardized. Otherwise, the data should be normalized. This applies if the range of quantity values is large (10s, 100s, etc.) or small (0.01, 0.0001).

If the quantity values are small (near 0–1) and the distribution is limited (e.g., standard deviation near 1), then perhaps you can get away with no data scaling. Predictive modeling problems can be complex, and how to best scale input data may not be clear.

If in doubt, normalize the input sequence. If you have the resources, explore modeling with the raw, standardized, and normalized data and see if there is a beneficial difference in the performance of the resulting model.

Smoothing

Smoothing of analog data is another data preprocessing technique to reduce noise and variability in continuous data by creating a smoother representation of the underlying trends or patterns. This technique applies to time-series data or any other analog data that exhibits fluctuations, irregularities, or noise that may obscure the underlying patterns or trends.

The primary goal of smoothing is to remove short-term, high-frequency fluctuations in the data while preserving the essential long-term trends or patterns. It can make the data more interpretable and suitable for further analysis, such as trend analysis, forecasting, or modeling.

We use several methods for smoothing analog data:

- **Moving average**: Moving average smoothing involves calculating the average value of data points within a sliding window or moving window of a specified size. The resulting smoothed data points represent the average behavior of the data over time. This method is effective at removing short-term fluctuations while preserving longer-term trends.

- **Exponential smoothing**: Exponential smoothing assigns exponentially decreasing weights to past data points, with more weight given to recent observations. It's particularly useful for capturing recent trends and is commonly used in time-series forecasting.

- **Low-pass filters**: Low-pass filters are mathematical filters that attenuate or reduce the amplitude of high-frequency components in the data while allowing low-frequency components to pass through. Common low-pass filters include Gaussian filters and Butterworth filters.

- **Kernel smoothing**: Kernel smoothing, also known as kernel density estimation, involves estimating the underlying probability density function of the data by placing a kernel (a smooth, symmetric function) at each data point and summing them to create a smoothed curve. This method is often used in non-parametric density estimation.

- **Savitzky-Golay filter**: The Savitzky-Golay filter is a type of polynomial smoothing filter that fits a polynomial to a moving window of data points and uses the polynomial coefficients to estimate smoothed values. It's especially useful for preserving the shape of peaks and valleys in data.

The choice of smoothing method depends on your data's characteristics and specific goals. Some methods may be better suited to remove certain types of noise or fluctuations, while others may be more appropriate for preserving certain features in the data.

Smoothing can be beneficial in various applications, including signal processing, financial analysis, and environmental monitoring, where noisy analog data needs to be cleaned and prepared for further analysis or modeling. However, it's important to balance noise reduction and preserve important details in the data, as excessive smoothing can result in the loss of relevant information.

Resampling

Resampling of analog data is a data preprocessing technique used to change the frequency or time intervals of a continuous data signal. This technique is commonly employed in various applications, including signal processing, time-series analysis, and data preparation for machine learning, to align data with a desired time or frequency grid.

There are two primary forms of resampling:

- **Upsampling (interpolation)**: Upsampling involves increasing the sampling rate of the data, which means adding more data points to the original dataset to represent the same signal with higher granularity. This is often done when you need to analyze or visualize the data at a finer time or frequency resolution. Common methods for upsampling include linear interpolation, spline interpolation, or Fourier-based techniques. These methods estimate the values of the new data points based on the existing data.

- **Downsampling (decimation)**: Downsampling involves reducing the sampling rate of the data, which means removing data points to represent the signal at a coarser time or frequency resolution. This is typically done to reduce the amount of data, especially in cases where the original data is too high-dimensional or noisy. Downsampling methods often include averaging or taking every nth data point, where "n" is the downsampling factor. For example, if you have data sampled every second and you want to downsample it to every minute, you would take the average of the 60 data points within each minute interval.

Resampling is useful in various scenarios:

- **Time-series analysis**: In time-series data, resampling can help align multiple time series with different sampling rates, making it easier to compare or model them.

- **Signal processing**: Resampling can be applied to analog signals to match the sampling rate of the recording equipment or to prepare signals for specific processing techniques.

- **Data preparation for machine learning**: In machine learning, resampling can change the temporal resolution of time-series data to make it compatible with certain algorithms or reduce computational complexity.

- **Data aggregation**: Resampling can aggregate data over larger time intervals, which can be useful for generating summary statistics or visualizations.

When resampling analog data, it's essential to consider the trade-off between temporal or frequency resolution and the potential loss of information. Up-sampling can introduce noise if not done carefully, and down-sampling can lead to information loss if critical details are discarded. The choice of resampling method and the new sampling rate should align with the specific objectives of your analysis or modeling task.

The distillation process

There needs to be a distillation process to achieve this data division. The distillation process reads all of the data generated by the machine. The distillation process then sends unuseful data to bulk storage and places useful data in the data lakehouse.

The best time to execute the distillation program is when the data is released from the machine. Also, the actual distillation of analog data can be done at either the data lakehouse level or the bulk storage environment level.

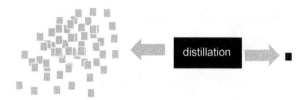

Figure 4-4. Analog data needs to go through a distillation process that separates useful from unuseful data.

What criteria does the distillation process use to determine which data will be selected and which will not be selected? The choice is made through a distillation algorithm. It is the distillation algorithm that reads the raw data and makes the determination of which path the data should take. So, exactly how does the distillation algorithm make this choice? Several ways.

Thresholds

Perhaps the most universal way the distillation process decides is by establishing one or more thresholds. Then, when a value that is read is beyond the threshold that has been established, the record is recorded as if it were an important piece of data. Or if the record that is read lies within the boundaries of the threshold, then the data is deemed unuseful.

Thresholds can be reset over time. Initially, the designer tries to establish the threshold(s) as meaningfully and as carefully as possible. A good source to turn to in establishing the thresholds is an experienced engineer who has worked with the data before. An experienced engineer knows what the thresholds ought to be. Or if there is no engineer available, the analyst sets the thresholds, monitors the results, and resets them soon after the first results start to come in.

Data characteristics

Another approach is to look for certain characteristics being measured and select the data based on the characteristics. As in the case of thresholds, the experienced engineer can best guide the analyst to what characteristics of data are of interest.

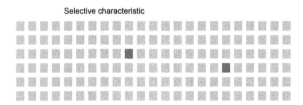

Selective characteristic

Figure 4-5. Choose only occurrences that have certain characteristics.

Timeboxing

Yet another approach is to use the technique known as timeboxing. On occasion, interesting data appears at certain times. Rather than look at the data itself, the analyst selects some likely period of time when interesting occurrences are likely to emerge and then selects all the data generated in this time frame.

The manual approach

There are undoubtedly many other approaches to selecting data that are useful for analysis and belong in the data lakehouse. But there is always the manual approach for distillation. The problem with the manual approach is it is:

- Expensive
- Laborious
- Error-prone.

For these reasons the manual approach should be the last resort, if nothing else works.

Parquet

When you need to store a large volume of data, such as less-than-useful analog data, store it in a Parquet database. The Parquet format stores data efficiently and should be the default choice for storing large amounts of data.

Post processing

When data is moved to bulk storage, that does not mean that it has been discarded. It merely means that it has been stored in a location where it can be accessed if needed later in time. If data is stored in bulk storage, it must be recognized that it can still be accessed, but accessing large amounts of data in bulk storage is slow and usually complex. And, of course, once the data that is desired in bulk storage has been located, it can be placed back into the data lakehouse.

Archiving the data lakehouse

As a final note, over time all data ages. As data ages, its probability of access and probability of usefulness decreases. For this reason, it is desirable to periodically archive data from the data lakehouse for bulk storage or elsewhere. Archiving old data is necessary and is healthy for the data lakehouse.

After the data that has been deemed to have business value has been located, it is placed in the data lakehouse.

CHAPTER 5

The Paradigm

You might have heard that there was first a data warehouse and then a data lake, and both had advantages and disadvantages. The data warehouse was good for structured data and the data lake was good for unstructured data. But the data lake just stores data and doesn't manage it. Then, there were critical business needs to have a solution that was the best of both worlds. There was a dire need to devise a methodology to extract valuable meaning from the data dumped into the data lakes. Over time, the data lying in the data lakes made it nothing more than a data swamp because the business kept dumping the data into it, and no one knew what to do with it.

Let me cover the data lakehouse in a practical way so that you can correlate it to the real world and with your actual business needs before you decide why and what exactly worked well with data lakehouse.

In almost every book, article, blog, and document, it has been written like "Data warehouse WAS," and "Data lake WAS" good for this and good for that, and "Data lakehouse IS" the best of both. This 'WAS' might give you a sense that those technologies are not around now and the data lakehouse 'IS' going to solve the purpose of both the data warehouse and the data lake in a single package of the data lakehouse.

But the fact is that both of these technologies of data warehouse and data lake are VERY MUCH THERE. They have not gone anywhere, and they are not 'WAS'. They are 'IS'. The data lakehouse provides a fabric to leverage these technologies together for all types of structured, semi-structured, and unstructured data.

The challenge with unstructured data

Bringing textual business data mainstream to actively participate in enterprise business decision-making is a challenge. Very few technologies can make or convert them to a structured format or to an analyzed format.

Still, unstructured data needs a variety of pre-processing before it is part of the ecosystem or part of the analyzable digital world. For example, scanned or printed documents might need OCR processing, a voice recording might need transcription processing, and an image needs another level of pre-processing to capture various parameters and metadata before it starts making sense for the respective business. A video to be used by a traffic police department might need different sets of metadata about the video for analytics. They may need to know who is violating or has violated the traffic rules or who committed a crime on the road. A video for a movie censor board needs different information and parameters. They might be interested in analyzing if there are violent or obscene scenes in the movie or the clip so that they can censor it for kids.

Similarly, video streaming in a manufacturing unit or warehouse may need different parameters captured for the necessary intelligence. They might want to see if the process is safe or if anyone on the shop floor may do some hazardous act and warn them to prevent an accident. A shop floor manager might want to see if any worker is working properly or if he is undergoing some mood swings like anger or argument with any worker, and so on and forth. Similarly, a chip fabricating and manufacturing company can use image processing intelligence to check the quality of the chips for any fault in the fabrication or printing. A printing company can use image processing to identify if there is any printing error or fault at runtime.

In many cases, intelligence in unstructured data can bring in tons of value to the business either at run time or at lateral stages, and the timeline and stages of usage are completely business-needs based. For example, a movie censor board doesn't need intelligence at run time. But a chip fabricating unit's quality department might need the intelligence and processing at run time. The pre-processing of required machine learning algorithms before the video or clip can bring some value to the business. Without this, the video might not have any meaning. In other words, if you want or try to analyze the video or the video clips, you may need to invest your own time sitting in front of the video or the video clip, watching the whole clip to find if there are any obscene shots in the video so that you can censor the movie for kids. Or you may need to sit in front of the live traffic camera streaming to catch a culprit or check if anyone is violating the traffic rules, etc.

Data warehouse, data lake, and data lakehouse myths

A data warehouse is a good choice for companies seeking a mature, structured data solution focusing on business intelligence and data analytics use cases. However, data lakes work for organizations seeking a flexible, low-cost, big-data solution to drive machine learning and data science workloads on unstructured data.

Suppose the data warehouse and data lake approaches aren't meeting your company's data demands, or you're looking for ways to implement both advanced analytics and machine learning workloads on your data. In that case, a data lakehouse is a reasonable choice.

A data lakehouse can be complex to build from scratch. And you'll most likely use a platform built to support open data lakehouse architecture. So, research each platform's different capabilities and implementations before procuring one.

Whichever solution you choose, it should meet your enterprise business needs. It should be simple to continuously and non-intrusively ingest all your enterprise data from various sources in real-time for data warehousing. It should be able to preprocess your data in real-time as it is being delivered into the data lake stores to speed up downstream activities.

So, the conclusion is that it all depends upon the need. If you need a data warehouse today, you can still go for a data lakehouse tomorrow. Or you can build a data lakehouse eventually on top of a data lake.

A data warehouse can come first and then the data lake, with eventually a data lakehouse on top of it. Or there is nothing wrong if you create a data lakehouse on top of your enterprise data lake, design your enterprise data warehouse on top of it, and even create various subject-oriented data marts.

Even within this development cycle of data warehouse and data marts, you can decide which way to go: top down or bottom up.

> *The data lakehouse is a data management paradigm over storage that can accommodate structured, semi-structured as well as unstructured data.*

It can also be achieved by applying a data warehouse-like data structure over comparatively low-cost and scalable data management and storage like a data lake. It enables Business Intelligence (BI) and Machine Learning (ML) operations to be easy, effective, and performant.

The architectural paradigm

The data lakehouse is built to house both structured and unstructured data.

The data lakehouse might use intelligent metadata layers that can be understood as "intermediary or a middle man" between the unstructured data and the data user. By identifying and extracting features from the data, it can effectively be structured, allowing it to be cataloged and indexed just as if it were relevant, tidy, structured business data that can now actively participate in the underlying business analytics for various decision supports.

The data lakehouse architectural paradigm is a data management and implementation methodology based on low-cost and directly accessible storage that also provides traditional analytical DBMS management and performance features such as ACID transactions, data versioning, auditing, indexing, caching, and query optimization.

The data lakehouse architecture can be implemented in many ways. It can help achieve many enterprise purposes if applied effectively and smartly. Here 'effectively' and 'smartly' have special meaning. We will see how it implies when it comes to enterprise-level implementations and usability.

Implementation methodologies

One implementation methodology is the one we discussed earlier in this chapter: Applying a standard and proven data warehouse data structure over a low-cost and scalable data lake. Another is using a low-cost storage and creating your own select intensive ecosystem for effective data management. A third is using the market's available OEM-based products or solutions for creating a data lakehouse.

There are other ways, which we will be discussing in further readings.

Scenarios of enterprise data lakehouse implementations:

1.   Green field data lakehouse implementation needs.

2. Data lakehouse implementation needs in an enterprise where the EDW (Enterprise Data Warehouse) already exists.

3. Data lakehouse implementation needs in an enterprise where the data lake already exists.

4. Data lakehouse implementation needs in an enterprise where data warehouse and data lake are already in place.

5. An enterprise with a data lake where business lost the track how to use the data lying in the data lake converted in a data sump.

Data processing stages

1. **Data processing for its quality**: The moment it comes to data quality, it reveals different facets of data quality assurance. Cleansing, profiling, massaging, standardization, aggregation, anonymization, filtering, augmentation, data provisioning, contextualization, and virtualization are all part of data duality actively or passively.

2. **Data pre-processing and data enablement for analytics**: Data enablement means making the data participate in business analytics. We know that a big portion of any enterprise data is semi-structured or textual. Before we make it available for BI and Analytics, it must be processed.

For example, we can't directly put effective analytics over legal agreements, corporate contracts, textual medical history narrations, discharge summaries, patent papers, voluminous research papers, emails, logs from different types of devices, customer feedback or review comments, internet posts, etc. Documents can be digital, hard copy, scanned images, videos, voice recordings, etc.

How can we analyze a hard copy of text like a legal agreement or contract? How can we use a textual PDF file for the purpose of analytics? How can a doctor's medical statement be directly analyzed? How can we compare two images of a national border that were taken at a gap of a few months to see and analyze if there is any knowingly or unknowingly activity by the neighboring country on the border? The answer to all the above questions is we need to pre-process all such data to make it analyzable.

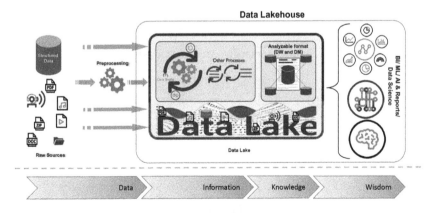

Figure 5-1. Data lakehouse architecture.

A data lakehouse designed for an enterprise should be simple, versatile, open, and collaborative. The versatility and simplicity of the underlying data lakehouse should reflect in your enterprise-level data engineering, data science and machine learning initiatives, real-time data streaming and applications, and enterprise-level business intelligence and analytics.

Since a data lakehouse is a paradigm, enterprise-level data management and governance make an enterprise data lake and data warehouse a real and effective data lakehouse. The data lakehouse has consumption capability and metadata management capability for structured, semi-structured, unstructured, and textual data.

In Figure 5-1, we can see that the sources can be raw, including any structured or semi-structured data, system and IoT device logs, and text, or any other form of unstructured data, such as video, audio, images, etc.

Data sources may need pre-processing like OCR, transcriptions, translation, conversion, metadata creation, and many other kinds of pre-processing required for different types of documents at the source.

A data lakehouse can be more versatile if we accompany the conventional data management and governance with modern Data Lakehouse Housekeeping™ methodologies, Data Future-proofing™, and successful implementation of FDM™ (Future-proof Data Management). I have discussed it for the first time in our book, "Building the Data Lakehouse". I will discuss these topics in much more detail for the benefits of all data lakehouse professionals who want to build a data lakehouse and implement a data lakehouse that is more open, versatile, and collaborative, yet very simple. This new, modern, innovative data management and governance methodology will help you build a better data lakehouse.

Analytical Workbench

Let's discuss the Analytical Workbench in detail.

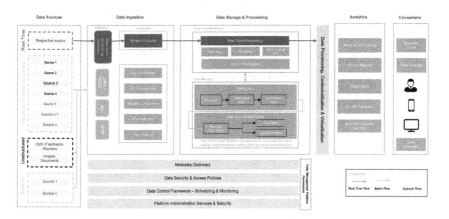

Figure 5-2. Data lakehouse Analytical Workbench architecture.

As mentioned earlier, the data lakehouse is a paradigm, and this paradigm has a purpose. The purpose is to give an enterprise a platform to analyze all types of data. The data warehouse only helps with the analysis of structured data. The data lake only helps with storing (and not using) semi-structured and unstructured data. The data lakehouse solves this critical problem of data. It becomes the guiding principle behind making the data meaningful by applying some processes over the data. It helps create an Analytical Workbench over the data store.

The phases of an Analytical Workbench can be classified in six parts:

1. **Data sourcing phase**. Data sourcing helps identify, classify, categorize, and segregate heterogeneous and/or diversified source systems. Data sources can be many or few. Some might hold semi-structured data like sensor logs or IoT devices, or many other system's continuous logs. It can be unstructured data like SMS, feedback, reviews, etc. Data sources can be internal or external. Data sources can be at diversified locations across cities or across the globe. Here in this phase, after identification, classification, categorization, and segregation, the actual data deep dive happens. Here, only pre-processing needs analysis is done. This is the phase when you decide whether a set of data or the data source is of any use. If it is of any use, what kind of use will it be, what sort of data does it bring in, and what sort of treatment does it need before ingestion? What is the state of the source or the legacy data? Is the effort required in its treatment worth the value it will ultimately add to the

business? Is it the only source for that specific set of data, or are there alternatives? Is the given source the primary, secondary, or tertiary source? What is the reliability index of the source in question? And so on.

2. **Data ingestion phase**. Data ingestion ingests the data from heterogeneous and diversified sources. It pushes it to the data storage and processing phase for transformation and storage to its desired target. Ingestion can have many interfaces like real-time streaming to handle data streaming from source systems in real-time. It can be JDBS- or ODBC-based interfaces. It can be API-based for data ingestion. It can be a secure FTP interface. Similarly, there can be many types of connectors for data ingestion: stream producers, DB connectors, API consumers, stream consumers, file watchers, and file parsers. It can have all the best ways to ingest the enterprise data to the ultimate storage system to create the enterprise data lakehouse.

3. **Data storage and processing phase**. Data storage and processing is the heart and soul of the overall Analytical Workbench. It will have transformation. It will have processing. It will have storage. The data architect will have tons of opportunities to use his/her experience and skills here to pick and

choose the best methodology to do it well for that specific business and enterprise needs. This is where we achieve the required data cleansing, profiling, and standardization. The target will be modeled, source and target mapped, and the associated transformation logic written. Business validation will be done. ETL and data transformation of all types of sources including semi-structured and textual data will be completed. Natural Language Processing (NLP) and/or textual ETL will also be considered in this phase only. Here, the architect should decide whether to do a top down approach or the bottom up approach. That is, whether the data warehouse needs to be created first and then the subject-oriented data marts, or the data marts first and then a consolidated enterprise data warehouse (the EDW). The Analytical Workbench gives ample flexibility to the data architect and the enterprise architect to choose the best possible option as per enterprise needs and business use cases. It doesn't restrict or limit the implementation methodology.

4. **Data analytics phase**. Data analytics is provisioned over and above the data storage. In this phase, all KPI-based reporting and dashboards are generated. Alerts and notifications are set and configured. AI and ML pipeline is created. In this phase only the

machine learning sandbox can be set up for further business research.

5. **Data consumption phase**. Data consumption by business users, data analysts, data scientists, etc., can be through mobile or desktop but only over the data analytics phases. They are the consumers of the artifacts created in the data analytics phases.

6. **Data management and governance phase**. Data management and governance phase includes the metadata dictionary creation, such as data access policy and data security. The controls like scheduling and monitoring are covered under this phase only. The whole workbench platform administration service and security is very much part of this phase.

The data transformation methodology is subjective and based on business needs and business use cases. For example, different business scenarios may lead to different ways of data ingestion. There can be a few cases where ETL is a best-fit method of data load. In other cases, only Extract, Load, and Transform (ELT) is the best method.

Let us discuss these two business scenarios to understand the needs of ETL versus ELT:

- An airport authority looks after over 100 international airports. Each airport has its own parking management system. Later, the airport authority wants to tap into the revenue leakage at various airports' parking by creating a centralized data warehouse. Here, doing transformation on the fly, just after the extraction, and before load is not recommended because all sources are spread across the country. To reduce the risk of unnecessary carrier load and to avoid any performance hit in the process, the transformation is needed after the data is loaded at the destination. The transformation after the load will be optimum performing and low cost in many ways. Hence, we can opt for ELT.

- A defence organization wanted a completely new development of all their applications. They have legacy applications on a monolithic architecture. They want to switch to a microservices architecture. However, there is a huge amount of data in the legacy environment. Once the microservices architecture is set up, the legacy data must be migrated to this new environment. The legacy and new enterprise applications are in the same city and network. So we can recommend ETL.

CHAPTER 6

The Governance

What is your dream home? Imagine its exterior, interior, layout, design, aesthetics, fences, connecting roads, architecture, and more. After the house is built, it must be maintained. An abandoned house starts looking like a haunted house after a few years. To maintain a house, we need excellent governance or housekeeping in place.

Where there is 'house', there is 'housekeeping'.

Housekeeping in terms of an organization also means recordkeeping, which facilitates productive work. Similar with a data lakehouse. We need to set up the housekeeping processes in place for a data lakehouse to be a data lakehouse forever, or else it will become a data lake (and haunt you like the haunted house). Data lakehouse housekeeping will help keep the data lakehouse in order year after year.

The housekeeping process distinguishes a data lakehouse from a data lake. As we know, a data lakehouse brings in the best of both a data warehouse and data lake.

Housekeeping helps you maintain the hygiene of the lakehouse. This specific housekeeping will help the data lakehouse maintain its value year after year. The housekeeping of the data lakehouse will help maintain the standard data acquisition, transformation, federation, and extraction processes, etc. It also helps regulate data management and governance in the lakehouse.

The kinds of housekeeping that keep a data lakehouse in order include:

- How will the data be integrated within the data lakehouse?
- How much interoperable should it be?
- How should the master reference within the data lakehouse be managed? How should the single version of the truth be managed?
- What privacy and confidentiality measures need to be considered within the data lakehouse?
- How can we ensure the data is relevant and usable way into the future?
- How do we do routine maintenance?

Let us discuss these kinds of housekeeping in more detail.

Data integration and interoperability in the data lakehouse

When it comes to data integration and data interoperability, these are the data aspects we can think of:

- Data acquisition
- Data extraction
- Data transformation
- Data movement
- Data replication
- Data federation

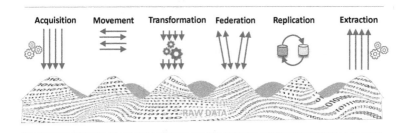

Figure 6-1. Data integration and interoperability in a data lakehouse.

Master references for the data lakehouse

Why master references in a data lakehouse? A data lakehouse is not data lake. In a data lake, you might not need a master reference. But as we have learned, a data lakehouse is the best of both data warehouse and data lake. Hence, a managed master reference becomes obvious.

A master reference is the reference of master data to manage shared data to reduce redundancy and ensure better data quality through standardized definitions and data values. It helps maintain a single version of truth across systems.

A clear distinction of shared data from across diversified source systems is a vital element for this portion of data lakehouse housekeeping.

Figure 6-2. Master reference layer in a data lakehouse.

Identifying such shared data will help maintain a single version of the truth across the data lakehouse. At one end, the data lakehouse will store data from heterogeneous sources; at the other, it will be the source of truth for various external but dependent systems. Various enterprise systems might extract required data periodically or regularly from the data lakehouse. In some cases, the data lakehouse might be the direct source of data for a few enterprise applications, including various analytics, data science, or cognitive tools/applications.

Once we identify master reference data, the layer needs to be structured and brought into use. Now, every system or data segment within and outside the data lakehouse (consumers of data lakehouse) should rely only on the reference and master data. It must be part of all ETL happening over the data lakehouse. Next comes the question of the precedence of references for master data. Solutions already exist and are used almost everywhere to create the master information repository. In this process, product owners or functional experts sit together to decide on the precedence of data to overwrite and/or update data into reference or master data. And application engineers need to write the rules engine needed for any master data overwrite/update or even delete (soft or physical delete).

Data lakehouse privacy, confidentiality, and protection

Data privacy, confidentiality, and protection are sometimes incorrectly diluted with security. For example, data privacy is related to, but not the same as, data security. Data security is concerned with assuring data confidentiality, integrity, and availability. Data privacy, by contrast, focuses on how and to what extent businesses may collect and process information about individuals.

> *You can say that privacy needs security — there is no privacy without security — but security doesn't need privacy.*

Data privacy, also called information privacy, refers to a specific kind of privacy linked to personal information provided to private actors in various contexts. Here, the definition of personal information is very subjective and may be defined differently in different contexts and domains. For example, personal information in social media might be your personal credentials, including name, sex, age, address, contact number, ethnicity, etc.; personal information in 'healthcare' might be a few vital EMR attributes of a patient like diagnosis, health conditions, vitals, treatments, etc.

Data confidentiality deals with protecting against the disclosure of information by ensuring that the data is limited to those authorized or by representing the data in such a way that its actual or original value remains accessible only to those who are entitled or possess some critical information (e.g., a decryption or decoding key for an encrypted or coded data). For example, a patient got treatment at a city hospital. The patient might not be interested in sharing his/her medical condition with anyone except his/her doctor who is treating him/her. Hence, it is the hospital's responsibility to maintain the confidentiality of the data of that specific patient. The application used to capture and store his/her data should be capable of handling this confidentiality. These data confidentiality rules apply to the data lake or the data lakehouse where that data ultimately resides within that enterprise.

Data protection is the process of safeguarding important data or information from corruption, compromise, or loss. The important information is very subjective. The definition of important information can be different for different organizations. Hence, the data protection process should be robust and comprehensive enough to address all required data protection to define enterprise data.

When doing data lakehouse housekeeping, be aware of the applicable data or information privacy policies and applicable confidentiality rules and regulations, and have a process to protect them. As mentioned, it is subjective and may be defined differently in different contexts and domains. Remember that a data lakehouse is very much part of the enterprise system. In fact, the data privacy, confidentiality, and data protection rules should be more comprehensively applied in a data lakehouse because a data lakehouse will accommodate data from hundreds of applications.

Data lakehouse routine maintenance

Most of the data lakehouse platforms are self-maintained, and their framework has robust data governance and management methodologies. But still, the part of data lakehouse housekeeping we should follow are the maintenance steps to keep the lakehouse in order:

Figure 6-3. Data lakehouse routine maintenance lifecycle.

Almost all the above steps have been discussed earlier in this chapter. The secret of data lakehouse maintenance is in its successful implementation. We should automate most of the processes using the provided utilities and tools within a data lakehouse platform. Meticulous planning and design of a data lakehouse supported by robust data lakehouse housekeeping will lead to great benefits.

CHAPTER 7

Data Future-Proofing

In terms of data, 'future proofing' can be defined as the process of anticipating the future and developing methods of capturing and arranging the data in a way that can minimize the gap due to missing or relevant data for data-driven research, correlations, trends, patterns, data supported evidence, past incidents and experiences, and many more. It can give you the confidence to prove and support your past data findings and help reduce the unwanted shocks and surprises that can cause business stress due to missing future-proof data.

All data of an enterprise might not be relevant for that enterprise years down the line. Organizational stakeholders are responsible for coordinating with data architects to decide the core entities and attributes that will be relevant and useful for business benefits.

Future-proofing data is a vast subject, but we will try to cover its broader aspects concerning building a data lakehouse.

Technology will keep evolving, employees and consultants may come and go, but accumulated data relevance will always be there for an enterprise. Next-gen business is all about data. All cognitive activities (including cognitive science) revolve around the data you accumulate. Whether it is healthcare, insurance, aviation, environmental, weather data, etc. But which data should be preserved, accumulated, stored, and saved for future use? All data might not retain its relevance in the future or far future. It will be a silly consideration that may lead to various problems, including but not limited to volume, policy breaches, misinterpretation, or misuse.

While considering future proofing of data, we must be sensitive about various aspects of data, including its relevance, grain, context, format, dimensions for different perspectives, future views, and viewpoints.

In this data context, a data view is what data you see, and a data viewpoint is where you are looking from. Data viewpoints focus on the business data for particular aspects of the business or the purpose. These aspects are determined by the concerns or business purposes of a stakeholder with whom communication takes place to future proof the data. Note that the data viewpoints may sometimes depend upon the stakeholders' perspectives and may be subjective. Therefore, it is a good idea to be little generic while deciding the prospective candidates (subject, entities, and attributes) for data future proofing.

Figure 7-1. Two different views of the same subject.

Capturing medical records is important. What are the benefits of historical medical records? It can help save human life. It can help in early diagnosis. It can help in medical research in many ways.

Take even the Covid pandemic scenario. We would have been far better if future proofing had been done for all the past medical records of similar epidemics or pandemics like Ebola, Avian Influenza, and Mers. A Covid vaccine would have been released much earlier, and lives would be saved.

However, handling medical records is a sensitive subject. Storing medical records at an application level has a different purpose than storing them in a data warehouse, data lake, or data lakehouse. While you bring a medical record to your data lakehouse, the purpose is to retain it for a different purpose than treating a patient. You certainly have the EMR application in place for the treatment of the patient that has all applicable privacy and confidentiality policies.

Once you capture this data into your data lakehouse, you might have captured it for medical research, early diagnosis, or preventive healthcare purposes. For these purposes, do you really need to know the name and Social Security Number of the patient who was diagnosed with Covid in 2021 and got treatment in a New York hospital? What you might need is the age (or age group), sex, hospital information, and medical conditions like symptoms, diagnosis, treatment, and the result of that treatment.

As another example of how data future proofing can help an enterprise protect itself from data vulnerability, imagine both personal and sensitive data. Personal data like name, address, medical details, and bank details, and sensitive data like race, political affiliation, religion, health, and criminal activity. The enterprise has been in business for more than two decades. Suddenly, another business from a different industry buys this company. What will be the future of all of this personal and sensitive data if data future proofing was not done?

Now let's discuss how the future proofing is done. We have divided "Data Future Proofing" processes into five different phases: identification, elimination, future proofing, organization, and storage.

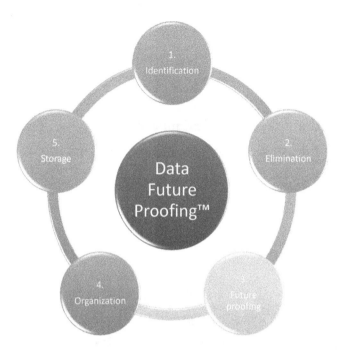

Figure 7-2. Five phases of "data future proofing".

Identification

Keeping the ultimate purpose of the future data in mind, identify all entities and attributes that will have relevance and are meaningful for various business needs and benefits. Such future-proof data purposes include but are not limited to analytics and research. You need to identify only the subject's future-proof entities and attributes. The subject can be your business domain like healthcare, insurance, aviation, manufacturing, education, transportation, hospitality, or retail.

In Figure 7-3 for example, the EMR might have hundreds of attributes in healthcare, but you might need just a few of them. The grain level of an EMR is every encounter of a patient, but for the future, you might need the extraction level from the disease, the number of patients diagnosed with that disease, gender, age group, cure status, and ultimate treatment.

Elimination

Eliminate all entities and attributes with no significance for any future analysis or research. Eliminate sensitive, future sensitive, and controversial data. Make a strategy to capture only meaningful data for future use. For example, in retail, how important is it to capture how many pairs of shoes a customer buys per order? Rather, we can focus on shoes' type, color, or design. This may give the perspective of fashion trend changes over time.

Figure 7.4 shows that only a few attributes should be sensitive and served with personal data. For example, a patient's medical condition and diagnosis can be sensitive if supported and linked to personal information like PID or SSN. Make a note of the data that will be sensitive or controversial only if linked to the original or relatable personal information like Name, SSN, PID (Patient ID), etc.

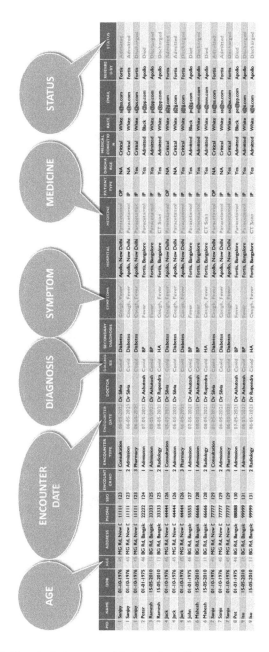

Figure 7-3. How to future proof data and attributes.

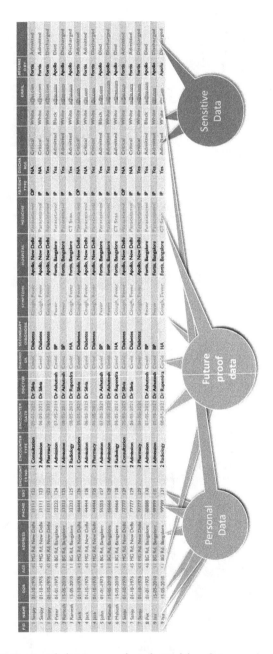

Figure 7.4. Personal, future proof, and sensitive data.

Future proofing

Phases 1 and 2 complete half of the future-proofing job. You identified only the data that will have relevance in the future. You eliminated all sensitive and controversial data. Yet if you have some data that you think might not be fair to expose for future use, or if it might be misleading or biased, anonymize it. With data anonymization, you retain the purpose yet don't expose the actual data.

In most business scenarios, a detailed level or the lowest grain level of data is not required for future use. The lowest cardinality of data is generally required in a transactional environment. Hence, we should judiciously decide the data extraction level or the grain level of data while future proofing your data. This will decide what the volume of your future proof data will be every year or every decade. The more the aggregation, the less the chance of personal and sensitive data being exposed. Data in its lowest grain level are the raw form of records that may incorporate all personal and sensitive data that are vulnerable if not handled responsibly. The data lakehouse has the lowest grain level of data, requiring more sensitivity to data future proofing features. In Figure 7.5, we may not care about Mr. Sanjay from New Delhi, but we may want to know the percentage of Covid-positive patients between 40 and 50 years of age.

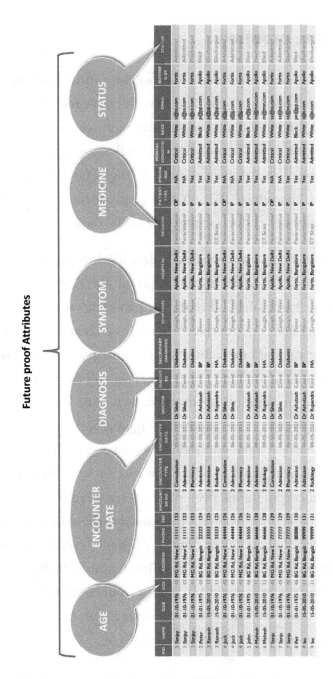

Figure 7.5. Future-proof attributes in an EMR data set.

So, it is clear and evident that we may not have any reason to store data with the lowest grain level. Data future proofing eliminates unnecessary data and reduces storage expenses, data vulnerability, and data complexity.

Next, we have to future proof the data capture cycle. Once you have decided on the grain and extraction levels, you write extraction rules, and then, based on the capture cycle, capture your future proof data. Your capture cycle can be daily, monthly, quarterly, or yearly. The mode of capture should be any supported storage mode, depending upon your destination storage system.

CHAPTER 8

Future-Proofing Data Management

Unlike your conventional organization of data in the destination system and like any special data management organization, we propose to have a separate Future-proof Data Management (FDM) layer in your destination data management, in this case, in your data lakehouse. FDM has nothing to do with MDM and CDM design or architecture. Conceptually MDM and CDM help manage enterprise data in efficient ways and help the business. Similarly, FDM will help manage future-proof data to be treated specially for future business benefits in efficient and strategic ways. The FDM layer should be treated differently and should be designed by following all five phases of data future proofing discussed in this section.

FDM is an implementation of an enterprise-wide system where the organization gets its historical information for any future use from a single managed place. A central repository is created, and all requests for future-proof data are satisfied from that one point.

Once it comes to storage of FDM, we recommend an open format, generic platform-based system, vendor-independent, non-proprietary infrastructure. This is because data future proofing is for the long term. Next in this phase is to ascertain the accessibility of the future proof data sets.

Who should have access to the data, who can have permission to insert, update, and delete any data in FDM? Then, discuss the availability of the FDM. It should not fall under 99.99999 availability.

Once you have ascertained accessibility and availability, storage upgradation is the last but not least important strategy under this storage phase. Make sure the storage upgrade is done for the FDM, where you keep all your future-proof data to be accessed seamlessly using the latest storage platform year over year and decades over decades. FDM is going to be a new, innovative and futuristic discipline in which the business and technology think together to preserve the past for the future.

A data lakehouse is built to house both structured and unstructured data. Therefore, it might use intelligent metadata layers that act as an intermediary between the unstructured data and the data user to classify the data into different categories. By identifying and extracting features from the data, it can effectively be structured, allowing it to be cataloged and indexed just as if it was analyzable and tidy structured data.

FDM in the cloud

In this cloud era, where an organization prefers to be on a private, public, or virtual cloud, for various reasons, we must admit that, at the end of the day, nothing is free on the cloud.

So even if a few 100 TB of enterprise data get accumulated year over year, and it is stored in the cloud, using cold storage that costs you very little like $0.004 per GB/month, and the retrieval rate is at $0.04/GB, then what would be the cheapest cost? Table 8-1 shows the approximate estimated cost of cloud storage before and after FDM implementation.

Cloud cost	Data volume in TB/ year	Cold Storage rate/ GB/ Month	Cold Storage cost/ year	Cold Storage cost in 10 years	Data Retrieval rate/ GB	Data Retrieval cost	Data Retrieval cost in 10 years	Total cloud cost
Before FDM	100	0.004	4,915	270,336	0.040	4,096	225,280	495,616
After FDM	10	0.004	492	27,034	0.040	410	22,528	49,562

Table 8-1. Approximate estimated cost of cloud storage before and after FDM implementation.

The storage cost will decrease significantly after implementing the FDM in your organization. You can reduce costs by almost 90% if FDM is implemented correctly.

The implementation strategy

We highly recommend implementing the FDM centrally and enterprise-wide for a better result, to avoid data redundancy and any conflicting data being referred into the FDM layer.

Create a strategy and roadmap to answer these questions to help yourself while designing the FDM layer for your enterprise:

- What do you want to achieve?
- What tasks can help you achieve it?
- What should be the order of those tasks?
- What benefits will you get out of it, and when?
- How much is it going to cost?

Purposes include:

- Facilitating future decision support
- Research, like market research, healthcare, or medical research
- Analytics, like statistical analysis, trend analysis, and future projection
- Various types of business learnings from past data.

Tasks include:

- Relevant and future-proof entity and attribute identification
- Anonymization (if required)
- Ingestion
- Transformation (if needed)
- Data quality
- Storage and preservation in future-proof formats.

The order is situational and completely based on business needs. Transformation might come during ingestion or after ingestion. Data quality task positioning is also situational. In some cases, it can be taken care of at the source, sometimes at the destination.

While we do future proofing of healthcare data, we might not need various attributes there or have already filtered out using our earlier discussed attributes by classifying attributes into three different categories: personal data, future-proof data, and sensitive data.

In most business cases, we eliminate personally identifiable and sensitive data while we design the FDM. In cases where we need to maintain those attributes for future use, we recommend applying anonymization for data privacy purposes, if allowed. We recommend it due to various reasons. One reason is the risk of exposure of sensitive data in the future or the cost over time due to preserving or storing such data and applying all sorts of data security over those data. In our chapter on data future-proofing, we have discussed various such use cases and the reasons behind such business use cases.

Benefits include:

- Reduced business liability over historical data
- Reduced storage due to eliminating personal and other sensitive data
- Reduced cost of storage in the cloud or on premise
- Reduced cost of data security
- Faster retrieval by keeping and maintaining readily accessible data format.

Costs include:

- One-time design cost
- Storage cost
- Maintenance cost.

Readily accessible data storage format

We recommend designing the FDM in a readily-accessible data storage format. That is ready to actively participate in the relevant business analytics at any time by avoiding vendor lock-in. A format that most of the analytics or visualization tools accept directly without further transformation in the data format, including .csv, parquet, and many such file formats, which are accepted by almost all analytics and visualization tools. They are convenient for AI- and ML-based advanced analytics as well.

No vendor lock-in

We discourage using any vendor lock-in-based product to store the FDM and FDM-related data. Avoid getting into vendor lock-in by using any Commercial off-the-shelf (COTS) product or other means. The FDM is the reference data for future usage, so any lock-in can be fatal and costly. You never know which product will go out of order or get obsolete. We don't want to put the FDM in trouble.

Auto pilot design

FDM needs to be designed in a way that is self-contained and maintained. Due to its transactional nature, maintenance overhead might be acceptable for current business data. FDM and data maintenance will bring in more costs. It can be a show-stopper for the business and cause further budget and funding challenges. We don't want any such hurdle that hampers the accumulation and ingestion of FDM. Any such break or unwanted interval in FDM data will spoil the purpose of FDM.

Autopilot means the sources and targets are pre-defined. Extraction level and transformation logics are pre-written. Jobs and trigger points are pre-set. There are no or minimal manual interventions.

Avoid multiple versions

Avoid multiple versions of the same type of data or information in the FDM, unless it is obvious and mandatory to have more than one version of a similar attribute or set of attributes. If you have more than one version, we recommend all versions be handled together regarding the associated data operations.

FDM as business mandate

FDM should be a business mandate for its successful implementations and executions. To reach this level, we must convey and discuss the benefits of FDM to the decision-makers. We should openly discuss FDM's financial and business benefits and futuristic nature. We should clearly tell them that if we don't implement FDM, the unnecessary and avoidable cost overheads will impact the bottom line.

FDM becomes necessary in this age where organizational growth is not limited to organic growth. Nowadays, organizations are not only growing organically. Inorganic growth is quite rampant. In fact, such a model of growth is working wonderfully for many enterprises that want faster growth and easy market coverage. The moment it comes to inorganic growth, the following factors become the root cause for data future-proofing:

- Business unit bifurcation or separation
- Product line segmentation
- Mergers
- Acquisitions
- Change in management
- Change in policies
- Change in business priorities, and so on.

CHAPTER 9

Leveraging Data Effectively

The data lakehouse paradigm was born due to limitations in the underlying architecture of the data lake. The challenge was how to leverage enterprise data effectively for the betterment of the associated business. People learned to ingest, stream, transform, load, and design optimized models. However, once people noticed that a large chunk of enterprise data remains unstructured, which could add much value to the business, they dumped this data into the data lake.

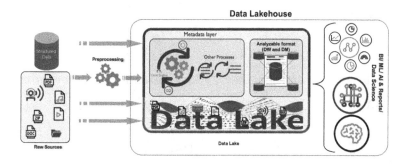

Figure 9.1. The data lakehouse architecture.

They kept dumping the data into the data lake, slowly losing context. At the same time, they devised a method to capture unstructured metadata through intelligent metadata layers. Ultimately, this became an intermediary between unstructured data and the data users.

Data models

A data model is an abstract that helps organize elements of data, and by following and applying certain formal techniques, a special relationship is established among those different elements of data, in some cases leading to different entities and attributes.

There are many data modeling myths around the data lakehouse that we will address in this chapter.

Let's start with these questions: Does a data warehouse need any sort of data modeling? And what about data lakes?

Yes to both! Yet, the nature of data modeling can be different in different cases. A data warehouse might need a dimensional modeling approach to design a select-intensive Online Analytical Processing (OLAP). The Operational Data Store (ODS) might need to be normalized and follow an ER modeling approach to cater to its respective purpose. A data lake can accommodate structured as well as unstructured data.

Let's review these different types of modeling that may exist in the data lakehouse:

- **Entity Relationship (ER)**. Represents the relationships between entities in a database through formal diagrams. Multiple tools and techniques exist to create ER data model visuals that can convey database design objectives.

- **Dimensional**. Includes star schema and snowflake designs.

- **Hierarchical**. Represents one-to-many relationships where each record has a single root or parent that maps to one or more child structures.

- **Relational**. Represents 50+ years old and proven Codd's rule that states for a system to qualify as a Relational Database Management System (RDBMS), it must be able to manage the database entirely through the relational capabilities. Relational data modeling doesn't require a detailed understanding of the physical properties of the data storage. In it, data segments are explicitly joined through tables, reducing database complexity.

- **Object-oriented**. Object-oriented data modeling got great engagement about 30-35 years back, while object-oriented programming was gaining more traction. The "objects" involved are abstractions of real-world entities. Objects are grouped in class hierarchies and have associated features. Object-oriented databases can incorporate tables and support more complex data relationships.

The above modeling types all emphasize entities/objects and their relationships. So, if the data lakehouse is the best of both worlds and those worlds need data modeling, how can we say that the data lakehouse doesn't need a data model? At the same time, we must note that the data lakehouse doesn't focus on only relational data. It also deals with non-relational data.

Hence, quoting that a data lakehouse always needs a data model is wrong. However, a data lakehouse needs a data model for relational data. Every phase of data management can have a different type of data modeling. For example, a data warehouse may need a dimensional model, an ODS, or a normalized ER model, and a data lake can have either or all of the above models due to its storage nature. In addition, a denormalized data model is not the same as a data model that has not been normalized, and denormalization should only take place after a satisfactory level of normalization has taken place and any required constraints or rules have been created to deal with the inherent anomalies in the design. For example, all the relations are in third normal form and any relations with joins and multi-valued dependencies are handled appropriately.

A database is a representation of facts. If there's more than one way to extract a single fact from the database, then there's a redundancy in it. Every redundancy can cause different anomalies in the data, which in turn causes bugs in the application. To avoid this, there's a process called normalization, which involves following sets of normalization rules to restructure the database to remove redundancies without losing the original facts. The traditional set of normalization rules are first, second, and third normal forms.

Denormalization means representing data in multiple ways to speed up queries without introducing inconsistencies. Examples of denormalization techniques include:

- Materialized views, which may implement storing the count of the "many" objects in a one-to-many relationship as an attribute of the "one" relation, and adding attributes to a relation from another relation with which it will be joined.

- Star schemas, which are also known as fact-dimension models, and have been extended to snowflake schemas.

- Prebuilt summarisation or OLAP cubes.

Remember this famous quote: *Normalize until it hurts, denormalize until it works* (that is, until performance becomes acceptable).

Key indicators or factors:

- One-to-one relationships
- Over normalized static data
- Tables with very few columns
- many-to-many join entities

Storage strategy

The data storage strategy in any paradigm is important for several reasons:

- **Cost**. The cost of storing data in the data lakehouse is very subjective and situational because it all depends upon the nature of the data and the business tolerance for data retrieval time. For example, if a business is ready to afford a retrieval latency of a few hours for any object store over two years old, and the business keeps it in cold storage, the cost will be extremely low. If the business needs data warehouse storage on an almost real-time or near real-time basis, the team will need to store the data warehouse in hot storage. And that will cost much more than cold storage.

- **Maintainability**. If data is in hot storage, the storage maintainability will be high. Cold storage will have respectively low or no maintainability.

- **Performance**. Storage decisions also depend on the acceptable latency or response time. For example, an airport authority maintaining the centralized data lakehouse of an eVPMS (electronic vehicle parking management system) might not be interested in looking at the previous year's parking data at its lowest grain level. In such a case, a proposal to push data older than one year to cold storage is fair enough. At the same time, only the current year's data should be in the hot storage, saving tons of revenue for the enterprise.

- **Lock-in**. We should note that the data lakehouse is not just for a year. It is a long-term enterprise application need. So, vendor lock-in might be tricky. Open-source solutions with enterprise support (if needed) are recommended to avoid such lock-in. Even if going for a commercial product, make sure that the migration from one product/platform to another is not cumbersome.

- **Compatibility with associated tools and technologies**. Any selected tool, technology, or platform should be compatible with other associated tools and technologies. We are in a continuously evolving technology world. Such due diligence will help in the long run for the betterment of the business.

So, whether it is cloud storage or on premise, the above key indicators will affect the storage strategy. Storage can be cold, warm, or hot. See Table 10-1 for a summary of these differences.

Type of Storage	Property		Availability	
	Cost	Time to retrieve	Cloud	On premise
Cold	Low	Slow	Yes	Yes
Warm	Medium	Moderate	Yes	Yes
Hot	High	Fast	Yes	Yes

Table 10-1: Differences among storage.

CHAPTER 10

Microservices Architecture and Security

Modernization may also include decomposing a monolith application into a set of independently developed, deployed, and managed microservices. The decoupled nature of a microservices environment allows each service to evolve with agility and independence. While there are many benefits for moving to a microservices-based architecture, there can be some trade-offs, too. As your monolithic application evolves into independent microservices, you must also consider the implications to your data architecture.

A lakehouse architecture embraces the decentralized nature of microservices by facilitating data movement. These transfers of data can be:

- Source systems to the data store, like staging to ODS
- between data stores like staging and ODS
- from data stores to data lake
- from data lake to data stores
- from data lake to data warehouse

- MDM to other data stores like data lake, ODS, and data warehouse
- Other data stores to MDM
- Data stores to other external systems, etc.

A microservices architecture-based development topped up with the following features brings in more value:

- Containerized
- With container orchestration framework
- Loosely coupled
- Convenient agile development
- Ease in CI/CD
- Highly secure
- Environmental consistency.

A microservices architecture-based development is loosely coupled, and scalable, and is faster to develop, deploy, and debug. It is technology- and OS-agnostic, and offers better data security.

So far, we have not been recommending a microservices architecture in data management projects like the data lakehouse. However, since a microservices architecture is standard across enterprise applications and the data lakehouse paradigm came into play, discussions around this data lakehouse versus microservices architecture became quite obvious. Primarily because of the demand and ask for the same in the industry.

In any microservices architecture, a few core components need to be discussed and addressed before getting into the details. We will also propose a microservices-based reference architecture for an enterprise-level data lakehouse. We will also support it with a use case of similar scale. See Figure 10-1.

A – **Purposed Application**. In an enterprise, multiple applications with almost similar workflows or functional requirements can exist. Can we categorize or group them? If yes, the next question will be, "What independent services can they be split into?" Indeed, each of those independent services can't directly cater to the 100% need of each application. But there is an efficient way to handle it. And that way is using a micro-repository based design. Within the microservices private database, we will have repositories that will help capture all the required properties for every application. For example:

- APIs app gateway
- Data pre-processing application
- Data ingestion application
- Data cleansing, profiling, and standardization application
- Data transformation application
- Scheduler and load application
- Reporting application
- BI and analytics application
- Dashboard and visualization application

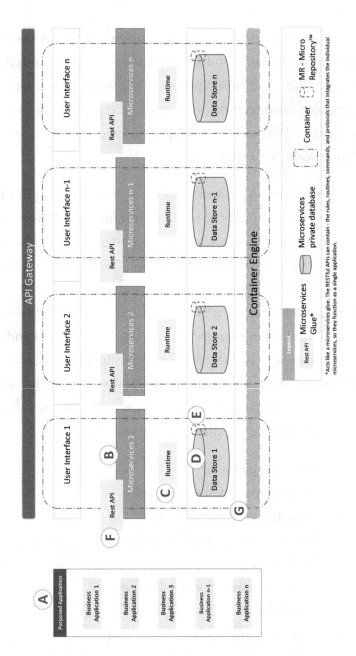

Figure 10-1. Reference Microservices Architecture with a new Micro Repository™ concept.

B – **Microservices**. Identification of independent microservices in an application or group of applications of similar types requires end-to-end understanding and visibility of the enterprise application's need. The purpose should be to identify independent services within the application that can help create loosely coupled services that can be glued together using Rest API for those services and complete the purpose of the integrated application in a better and more efficient way than a monolithic architecture. Containerization and its management and orchestration can be an option for a better and seamless integrated and managed environment. A secure environment can be assured by leveraging widely used API-security standards. Examples in the data lakehouse are:

- Microservices for the data lake
- Microservices for the data warehouse
- Microservices for each subject oriented data mart
- Microservices meant for different ETL or ELT jobs or workflows, based on different sources and different targets (very much subjective)
- Reporting microservices
- Advanced analytics microservices
- Dashboards or insights creation and publication microservices, etc.

C- **Microservices Runtime**. Microservices Runtime is optimized for execution within a container. You can run a microservice or a set of related microservices in a container. Even VMs might not be needed. A container includes configuration, enabling you to deploy the same configuration anywhere.

D – **Microservices Private DB**. Each microservice can have a private database to store the required data to implement the business functionality. A given microservice can only access the dedicated private database but not the databases of other microservices. You might have to update several databases for a single transaction in some business scenarios. In such scenarios, the databases of other microservices should be updated through its service API only (not allowed to access the database directly). Any deviation to the above statement should be considered a work around and not the standard.

E – **Micro Repository™**. Micro Repository is a special-purpose productization paradigm for the creation of multipurpose microservices. It helps use common microservices to cater to more than one integrated application within the enterprise. The underlying repository consists of system references, parameters, rules, commands, and formulas that need to be passed at runtime for different applications.

F – **Rest API as a glue**. When a business capability is implemented as a service, you need to define and publish the service contract. We need a capability that deals with

REST as a first-class citizen. Since we build microservices on top of the REST architectural style, we can use the same REST API definition techniques to define the contract of the microservices. Therefore, microservices define the service contracts using the standard REST API definition languages, such as Swagger and RAML.

G – **Container and Container Engine**. An open-source container engine lets developers and system administrators deploy self-sufficient application containers in various environments. Container provides a great way to deploy microservices while addressing the requirements. The key steps involved are as follows:

- Package the microservice as a container image.
- Deploy each service instance as a container.
- Scale it according to the number of container instances.

Building, deploying, and starting a microservice will be much faster as we use containers. In general, a container is much faster than a regular VM.

Micro Repository™

Primarily, this topic in this chapter is for those who understand the repository design patterns even at a high level, if not in depth. The first thing to remember about any design pattern is that design patterns do not depend on a specific technology, framework, or programming language.

In software engineering, a design pattern is a reusable solution to a general problem occurring in a given context in software design. A design pattern is not a design that is directly transferred into code.

Repository patterns separate the data access logic and map it to the business entities in the business logic. Communication between the data access logic and the business logic is done through interfaces.

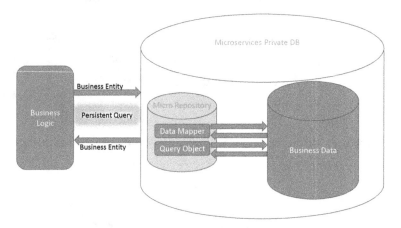

Figure 10-2. Repository pattern and the micro repository.

To put it simply, the repository pattern is a kind of container where data access logic is stored. It hides the details of data access logic from business logic. In other words, we allow business logic to access the data object without knowing the underlying data access architecture.

The separation of data access from business logic has many benefits:

- Centralization of the data access logic makes code easier to maintain
- Business and data access logic can be tested separately
- Reduces duplication of code
- A lower chance of making programming errors

In a nutshell, it is a technique to implement microservices within microservices. To understand it well, let us assume we have many ELT workflows due to a data lakehouse project for a National Airport Authority (NAA). There are over 100 airports under that national airport authority. Also, assume that the Airport Authority as a subject wants to create a central enterprise data lakehouse for eVPMS (Electronic Vehicle Parking Management System) to tap any revenue leakage across these diversified location-based airports across the nation. It was also purposed to cater to all users' grievances related to overcharges or any in-appropriate charges. As a national authority of the nation's airports, the airport authority wants the solution on a high-priority basis.

Sr#	Category	No. of Airports	Vehicle entering airport
1	Category 1	1	20,000 / day
2	Category 2	9	10,000 / day
3	Category 3	10	5,000 / day
4	Category 4	15	3,000 / day
5	Category 5	65	1,000 / day

Table 10-1. Airport relevant volumetric.

As per the use case, we understand that there can be many cases where the airport eVPMS application or the system for this specific purpose implemented by the concessionaire are in different states like cloud, on-prem, standalone, or manual. So, in any such scenarios, we can have data objects from:

- Cloud sources with eVPMS hosted on cloud
- On premise sources
- Standalone sources
- Manual sources where the tickets issued are paper/slip based, and no direct machine is involved.

All the above sources are country-wide diversified airports sources.

We understand here that whether the data comes from cloud, on premise, standalone, or a manual system, it finally gets ingested to the data lake's target staging as part of the extract and load. So, in such cases, we may not need separate microservices for cloud sources, on-premise, standalone, and manual sources. Rather, we can leverage the power of the Micro Repository, which can parameterize any information that makes the microservice a multipurpose microservice.

You can see in Figure 10-3 that no separate ingestion microservices are needed for different source data from diversified sources, whether it is the extract, load, or transform microservices. Any such deviation in the variable parameters is handled using this new paradigm of the Micro Repository™. We simply put a layer between the business logic and the microservices' private databases, which we call the micro repository layer of the database, that contains all the repository information needed by the microservices to act accordingly.

Once you closely observe the overall implementation of the data lakehouse, you realize it is tricky to implement the microservices architecture end-to-end. You can certainly implement microservices, but it will always be a partial implementation of the microservices architecture. So take the call judiciously. Evaluate how much impact the implementation of microservices architecture has on your data lakehouse project. Such decisions are very situational and depend greatly on the nature of the business needs and other parameters that vary from business to business.

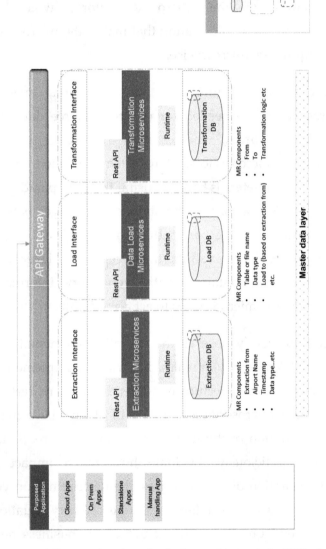

Figure 10-3. Microservices-based solution architecture for ELT of eVPMS centralized data lakehouse as per this use case.

Security in the data lakehouse

Security in the data lakehouse is an important topic. Due to its nature of enterprise-wide implementations, its capability of storing, preserving, and handing all types of data, including structured, semi-structured, and unstructured data. That means we aim to keep all kinds of enterprise data in the enterprise data lake underneath the lakehouse. Now, it is more vulnerable to theft, cyber-attacks, and malware.

Security at rest and security in motion are important apart from network-level security, system-level security, database-level security, and application-level security. We suggest security at all levels, including:

- Data security, including data security in motion and data security at rest.

- Application security, including a secured application architecture and a standard, leakproof, and non-vulnerable coding practice.

- Hardware security, including device and equipment level security, and network and communication channel-level security.

- Physical security, including tailgating prohibition, accompanied guest, and CCTV surveillance.

- Business security, including business policy for security like a no tailgate policy, mandatory escorting rules for visitors, and organizational guidelines.

CHAPTER 11

Bulk Storage

There is no question that fresh, up-to-date data is the backbone of analytical processing. Accessing the data needed for analysis quickly and accurately is at the heart of the data lakehouse. However, underlying fast and easy data access is a necessary and unglamorous type of storage that complements the data lakehouse. That storage is called bulk storage. Building a data lakehouse without a complementary bulk storage component is a mistake.

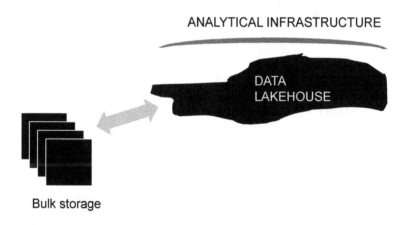

Figure 11-1. Bulk storage is a natural complement to the data lakehouse.

What is bulk storage?

Bulk storage is storage that is designed to house a large amount of data inexpensively. For all practical purposes, bulk storage can store unlimited data. In almost every circumstance, bulk storage is accessed sequentially. This implies that searches of bulk storage can be time-consuming and expensive. And the more bulk storage there is, the longer the searches of bulk storage take.

Another trait of bulk storage is that it is designed to last for a lengthy period of time. Stated differently, bulk storage does not physically degrade or corrode easily over time. This is important because bulk storage becomes the storage mechanism for archival data. Any storage media that easily corrodes over time is not fit for usage as bulk storage.

Probability of access

The dividing line between what data goes into bulk storage and what data goes into the data lakehouse is the probability of access. Data with a high probability of access goes into the data lakehouse. Data with a low probability of access goes into bulk storage.

The algorithms used to predict probability of access need to be checked and rechecked. And over time, these algorithms change.

The value of bulk storage

What benefit does bulk storage have to the data lakehouse? The answer is that by removing data with a low probability of access from the data lakehouse, analysis in the data lakehouse becomes much more efficient. In addition, removing low probability data from the data lakehouse means that data in the lakehouse is easier to find. A third benefit is that the cost of storage in the data lakehouse is reduced. As a rule, it is cheaper to store data in bulk storage than it is in the data lakehouse.

Algorithms

We apply the algorithms that predict the probability of access of data before data enters either the data lakehouse or bulk storage. These algorithms are complex and change over time. It is wise for the analyst to experiment with the algorithms as data is first placed in the data lakehouse. Furthermore, the actual queries that are done need to be monitored to ensure the accuracy of the algorithms.

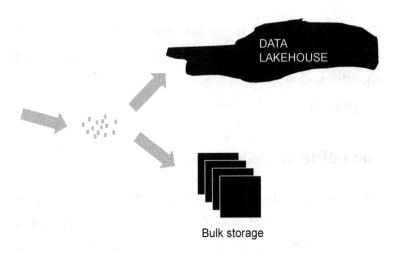

Figure 11-2. Data is divided based on the probability of access.

So what happens if we place data in bulk storage that is needed in the data lakehouse? It is a simple (and time-consuming) matter to scan the bulk storage and place the needed bulk storage in the data lakehouse. Of course, reading and selecting data in bulk storage is not an easy exercise. In any case, such a scan consumes a huge amount of resources. A sequential search of bulk storage is never fast and efficient.

Archiving data

In addition to moving data from bulk storage to the data lakehouse, a reverse move is also possible. Periodically, data can be removed from the data lakehouse to bulk storage. This process is called the archiving of data.

Archiving of older data is a feature that belongs in every data lakehouse.

If the interchange of data from bulk storage to the data lakehouse is done frequently, this is a sign of the algorithms' ineffectiveness in determining the probability of access.

Incidental indexes

To mitigate the difficulty and expense of accessing bulk storage, it is possible to create what can be called an "incidental index". In most cases, an index is created to find a particular record of data. An incidental index is merely used to find whole classes of data, rather than a particular record.

Typical incidental indexes might be on year. When searching on bulk storage, it is much easier to access a year's worth of data than to access the entire bulk storage. Another possibility for an incidental index might be geography. It is much easier to search activity that happened in Texas than to search all the data in the United States, for example. The incidental indexes are used to qualify whole sections of data rather than to look for a single record. The result is a much more efficient usage of bulk storage.

Analytical processing against bulk storage

Can you do analytical processing against bulk storage?

The answer is "yes". But it is time-consuming, complex, and expensive to do. Bulk storage is not designed for analytical process.

Asking whether you can do analytical processing against bulk storage is like asking if you can pull your hogs to market using a Ferrari. It is certainly possible to pull your hogs to market with a Ferrari. But that is an improper use of a Ferrari. Many better vehicles can be used to pull your hogs to the marketplace.

Platforms

Should bulk storage be on the same platform as the data lakehouse? The answer is, "It depends." There are cases where storing bulk storage on the same platform as the data lakehouse is perfectly acceptable. There are also cases where storing bulk on the same platform is not appropriate. It simply depends on the platform, the cost of storage, and the size and probability of bulk storage access.

CHAPTER 12

Archival Data

All data ages over time. As it ages, it becomes less useful to the organization. Data in the data lakehouse is no exception. For this reason, a data lakehouse needs to periodically purge the data that is no longer useful from the data lakehouse. However, the data does not actually need to be deleted. It merely needs to be placed in a location where it is less expensive to store it and where it is still available if needed.

The only difference in the need to reduce the data in the data lakehouse is the rate at which the data value decreases inside the data lakehouse. Some data ages quickly, other data ages less quickly. And as data ages, its value and its probability of access decrease.

There are lots of good reasons for purging less than useful data. One reason is that moribund data hides useful data. Another reason is that older data mixed with current data makes the analysis of current data more complicated. Yet another factor is the cost of storage. If an element of data has no usage, then that data costs money for which there is no return.

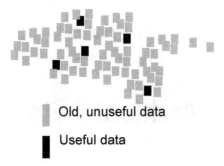

Old, unuseful data

Useful data

Figure 12-1. There are very good reasons for archiving data from the data lakehouse.

The archiving algorithm

We remove data from the data lakehouse by executing an archiving algorithm. Most archiving algorithms are simple. The algorithm has a date before which the data stays in the data lakehouse and after which the data is moved to archival storage. In almost every case, the archived data is moved to bulk storage to archive the data. On occasion, there may be other criteria for archiving data. However, far and away, the primary criteria for archiving data is the comparison to a date that resides in the data in the data lakehouse.

The archival algorithm normally operates based on time comparisons of the date in the archiving algorithm to time in the data lakehouse. The comparisons can be against the time of the execution of a transaction, against the time a record was created, or other measurements of time.

As a rule, many different measurements of time exist in the data lakehouse.

Archiving the analytical infrastructure

When we archive data for bulk storage, the analytical infrastructure may or may not be archived. If we determine that data must move to bulk storage and the analytical infrastructure needs to hold that data, then the reference to the data is changed from the data lakehouse to the bulk storage.

However, if there is no need to hold the reference to the data in the analytical infrastructure, the reference data in the analytical infrastructure can either be deleted or archived.

It is noteworthy that both summarized data and detailed data can be archived. In some cases, detailed data is archived and summary data may remain in the data lakehouse. On other occasions, both detailed and summary data can be archived. It is also noteworthy that the algorithms governing how data is summarized should also be archived.

At a later point in time, the analyst may need to determine exactly how those summarizations were made. The documentation of the summary algorithm should include both the actual summary algorithm itself and the selection criteria for what data has been summarized.

Moving data back to the data lakehouse

Occasionally, data must be moved back to the data lakehouse from archival storage. It is time-consuming to search for archival storage and return the necessary data. But archival storage can be searched and data can be returned from bulk storage to the data lakehouse. If data has to be returned to the data lakehouse frequently, we should adjust the archiving algorithms.

External data

In addition to archiving detailed and summary data, it occasionally makes sense to archive other external data that may be relevant to the data lakehouse. Typical external data that may be useful includes such things as:

- The year-to-year inflation rate
- The year-to-year average interest rate
- The year-to-year GNP

And so forth.

A good source of this kind of data is the Bureau of Labor and Statistics. The external data is often useful when comparing data over lengthy periods of time. Having them stored and available in archival storage may greatly help the data analyst.

Probability of access

If there is any over arching issue that separates archived data from active data, it is that data that has a high probability of access belongs in the data lakehouse and data that has a low probability of access belongs in archival storage.

CHAPTER 13

The Analytical Infrastructure

The analytical infrastructure is an extremely important component of the data lakehouse. In fact, a data lakehouse without an analytical infrastructure is not really a data lakehouse at all.

There is a very good reason why the analytical infrastructure is so important. The analytical infrastructure provides guidance as to what data is where in the data lakehouse. In short order, a data lakehouse starts to contain wide and diverse data. Furthermore, there is a lot of data in the data lakehouse. Because of this volume and diversity of data, it is very easy for the analyst to become lost or confused about the data that resides in the data lakehouse.

The analytical infrastructure provides a roadmap as to what data is in the data lakehouse, where to find that data, and how the data relates to each other.

To use an analogy, suppose you wanted to drive from the East Coast to the West Coast. A map would help make such a trip. You will probably never get from Florida to

Los Angeles without a map. And if by some chance you do, it will certainly not be a short and efficient journey.

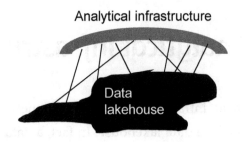

Figure 13-1. The purpose of the analytical infrastructure is to open up the world of the data lakehouse to the analyst.

There are many reasons for the complexity of the analytical infrastructure. However, the primary reason is that the analytical infrastructure must encompass three different worlds. The analytical infrastructure must accommodate structured, textual, and analog/IoT data. Each of these forms of data creates its own separate domain of data. The problem is that these different domains of data are extremely different. It is like trying to merge Antarctica, the Sahara desert and the jungles of the Amazon together. These places are all part of the planet earth, but they are very different from each other.

Metadata

The analytical infrastructure is made up entirely of metadata. But the metadata representing structured data is very different from the metadata representing sent textual data. And the metadata representing textual data is very different from the metadata representing analog/IoT data.

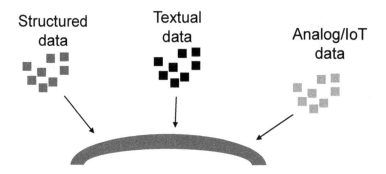

Figure 13-2. There are a few basic similarities in the metadata from these three different universes. But there are many, many differences.

The structured domain

The metadata of the structured environment is the metadata that most people are familiar with. This metadata includes:

- A data model
- Data Definition Language (DDL)
- Definitions of data.

The data model describes the data that forms the backbone of structured data. The definitions of the data include the formal definition of what is encompassed and what is not encompassed by any given element of data.

The textual domain

The metadata for the textual data component of the data lakehouse includes:

- The ontological description
- The taxonomical description
- Inline contextualization definitions.

The ontology contains the classifications of all data encompassed by the enterprise doing textual analytics. The taxonomy includes the classifications of the words used in a single component of the enterprise's business. The ontology contains one or more taxonomies. Inline contextualization contains the syntactical structures found within the text itself.

The analog domain

The metadata that is important for the analog/IoT environment is the definition of the algorithms that determine how to separate the analog data into useful and unuseful categories. In addition, the archiving algorithms are included in this metadata.

The data lineage domain

The fourth component of the analytical infrastructure is that of the lineage of data. The lineage of data includes the description of the flow of data, the algorithms used for altering the data, and the algorithms used for determining what data has been selected and what data has not been selected for the flow of data. In addition, data lineage also includes information about the scheduling of the flow of data, the volumes that are flowing, and so forth.

Data relationships

One of the most important components of the analytical infrastructure is the data relationships that are contained or implied in the infrastructure. The data relationships are important to the analyst because it is the relationships that determine how data can be combined and compared. Combining data is at the heart of analytical processing. One of the challenges of using data relationships is that they are often imprecise. The analytical infrastructure helps to clarify what those relationships actually are.

Making the matter of data relationships complicated is the fact that the data lakehouse contains both detailed and summary data. Data relationships start to become really complicated when the detailed data is mixed with the summary data.

Understanding the relationship between detailed and summary data requires including the algorithms used to calculate the summary data.

Two kinds of relationships in the data lakehouse are internal and external.

An internal relationship exists within the confines of a domain. For example, there may be a relationship between customer and orders within the domain of structured data. And within the textual domain, there may be a relationship between a customer's opinion and a product's usage. Within the analog domain, there may be a relationship between the output of a machine and the quality of the output. Internal relationships do not cross the different domains.

Occasionally (not frequently), there may be relationships across domains. In this case, there is a relationship from structured data to textual data. Or there may be a relationship between textual data and analog/IoT data.

For an external relationship to exist across multiple domains, one or two common data elements must exist across the different domains. Unfortunately, this is normally not the case. For example, there is no way to connect the opinion of car owners about their vehicles with the sale of gasoline. There is no common data connector. But suppose customers' opinion about the food found in a restaurant is compared to the sales and revenue of the restaurant. The location and name of the restaurant can be connected.

Loading the analytical infrastructure

It is noteworthy that we load the analytical infrastructure the same time as the data lakehouse. Furthermore, the analytical infrastructure is maintained and updated simultaneously with the data lakehouse.

CHAPTER 14

Understanding Data Lakehouse Data

A key component for using the data lakehouse data for analytical processing is to understand the data. It does not matter how the data lakehouse is being built, whether it is loaded in an organized manner or the data is just thrown into the environment, understanding the data is critical. This is important whether the data is used by analytics developers or in a self-service mode used by data scientists to create KPIs and analytics. Knowing the data is important for both structured and unstructured data, including equipment data from instruments, sensors, meters, data transmission, and other Internet of Things (IoT). Unstructured data may also include text data found in all types of documents and system text fields.

Understanding data in the data lakehouse is usually the responsibility of the data governance organization, which ensures that users of reports, dashboards, and visualizations can understand and trust the data for analytical purposes. They know what they are using, that it is the correct data field, and is in good standing for their analytics.

To find and use data lakehouse data accurately, users need to know about the data including its metadata. Accurate, trusted data can unite every person, team, and system across the organization. There are data governance tasks to vet, evaluate, and document critical metadata that is part of the data lakehouse.

Data definitions

We need to write data definitions in business terms, with ranges of data, formats (patterns), formulas, and examples to help the user ensure the right data is being pulled into their reports, metrics, and visualizations. Data definitions are part of a data catalog, which can also include data classification, compliance regulations, and data quality rules, which are also important for using the correct data.

Data classifications

Understanding the data classification of each data field is used to determine how to use and protect data that is populated in the data lakehouse. This includes the classifications of:

- **Restricted**. Data whose unauthorized access or loss could seriously or adversely affect your organization, a partner, or the public.
- **Protected**. Data that should be protected from general access.
- **Confidential**. All other non-public data not included in Restricted or Protected classes.
- **Public**. Data that can be released to the public.

Compliance regulations

Understanding applicable compliance regulations is important to understand what can be used and how to protect this data based on regulations that apply to specific data. Data compliance regulations are established by the governments, including:

- **CCPA** (California Consumer Privacy Act). Guidelines to businesses on how to inform consumers of their rights under CCPA, how to handle consumer requests, how to verify the identity of consumers making requests, and how to apply the law as it relates to minors.

- **GDPR** (General Data Protection Regulation). Guidelines for collection and processing of personal information of individuals within the European Union (EU).

- **FERPA** (Family Educational Rights and Privacy Act). Protects the privacy of student education records.

- **HIPAA** (Health Insurance Portability and Accountability Act of 1996). Provides data privacy and security.

- **HITECH** (Health Information Technology for Economic and Clinical Health). Title XIII of the American Recovery and Reinvestment Act of 2009. Updated HIPAA privacy and security with new areas of information breaches, audits, complaint processes, and enforcement.

- **Omnibus Rule**. Health Information Technology for Economic and Clinical Health (Title XIII of the American Recovery and Reinvestment Act of 2009).

- **PII** (Personally Identifiable Information). Any information connected to a specific individual that can be used to uncover that individual's identity, such as their Social Security Number, full name, or email address.

- **PHI** (Protected Health Information). Health or medical information in oral, written, or electronic format that can be uniquely identified or linked to a specific individual.

- **EPHI** (Electronic Protected Health Information). Requires covered entities (health plans, health care clearinghouses, and health care providers) to implement certain administrative, physical, and technical safeguards.

- **SOX** (Sarbanes-Oxley Act). Protects shareholders and the public from accounting errors and fraudulent practices in enterprises and improves the accuracy of corporate disclosures.

Data quality rules

Understanding the quality of data is important for users to know if the data is good enough to use for analytical processing. The user needs to know if the data is accurate, fully populated, partially populated, or of poor quality, helping users determine whether they should use this data for analytical purposes and decision-making.

The importance of data quality is critical, as poor-quality data can result in incorrect conclusions, inefficient operations, and a lack of trust in the information provided by an organization's application systems, and the data feed into the data lakehouse from those systems.

Data governance team members can develop data quality rules to apply to the data to check for the quality areas that are key to their organization. These consist of:

- **Data accuracy**. Valid data values that are populated in the data field and can be used as a reliable source of information. A critical component of data quality that can cause negative results when used for reporting, dashboards, or analytical processing is if the data values are inaccurate or even if some are inaccurate.

- **Data completeness**. A measure of essential information in a data set or model. Data is considered complete if it is without missing information. Many missing data values could make the data field unusable for analytical purposes.

- **Data uniqueness of business keys**. Important to be able to ensure that data is correctly linking to other sets of data.

- **Consistency of data**. The population of consistent data in a data field to ensure it is valid to compare data values within that data field.

- **Out-of-range data**. The existence of data values that are out of the range of valid domain values for this data field, which may cause this data field to be unusable for analytical purposes.

- **Format and patterns**. Refers to the use of standard formats and patterns in each data field to enable the user to compare, aggregate, and filter using data fields that have established patterns.

- **Data integrity**. Refers to the accuracy and consistency of data over its lifecycle. Data integrity describes data that is maintained as complete, accurate, consistent, and safe throughout its lifecycle. Data that is compromised can not only be unusable for users' analytics, but data loss can also harm the organization. Rules and procedures are applied at different levels to include application developers, database administrators, auditors, and the processing of periodic risk controls to ensure the integrity of data remains intact.

Another component of understanding data lakehouse data is to evaluate the data and the processing of data continually. Areas to evaluate include:

- **Data freshness**. How up-to-date the data is in the data lakehouse. Data is considered fresh if it provides the world as it is right at this moment. Recently refreshed data is considered more accurate, and, therefore, more valuable. Different types of data can have different requirements for data freshness. It might be sufficient for daily or even weekly or monthly loads for data that does not change frequently, but some data is needed hourly or even in real-time. Stale data is data that is out-of-date, obsolete, or no longer accurate. Stale data often occurs when an update or refresh process fails, is delayed, postponed, or is not performed regularly. Metrics to consider for evaluating data freshness are:

a. **Timestamps and collection frequency.** Every record is associated with a timestamp (usually date and time stamps) indicating when it was generated, collected, or pushed into the data lakehouse. The closer the timestamp is to the present time, the fresher the data.

b. **Latency and processing time.** Refers to the delay before a transfer of data begins following an instruction for its transfer.

c. **Batch-driven versus event-driven pipelines.** Batch-driven ETL is a common method for processing large volumes of data. Data is collected and processed in batches, typically at scheduled intervals, such as daily, weekly, or monthly. Batch processing enables organizations to process large volumes of data, minimizing the impact on the production systems since these usually process at times when the production systems are down. Event-driven processing is the method for processing data in real-time. Data is processed and loaded into the data lakehouse as it is generated, allowing for immediate processing, loading, and analysis using this data.

- **Data decay and relevance**. Refers to data becoming less accurate or less relevant over time. Organizations that do not update their data frequently may chase wrong opportunities or make decisions based on outdated information.

- **Growth (or decline) of records**. Refers to the expected trends in the number of rows in the tables, as well as increases or decreases in volume. We should evaluate the data for possible issues if tables do not grow (or decline) at the expected rate. This could indicate data issues, including processing failures, unexpected data values not correctly handled, missing reference table values, and missing links to other tables.

- **Usability of data**. Refers to what data, how it can be used, and why. The definitions provided by the data governance team, with the help of the business community and IT, should include a discussion on how and what to use this data for. The data might include flags or indicators to simplify the data queries. It can be a date with the time embedded, impacting how to use this data. The data can be set to a type of char or varchar where special characters (found in foreign names) can cause issues with the data.

- **Patterns of data.** Refers to the standard format or patterns found in data, including telephone numbers, Social Security Numbers, Zip Codes, FEINs, State Tax IDs, account numbers, and part numbers. Data with a set pattern can be evaluated for issues or changes to identify possible issues in data entry or data migration processes from external sources that need to be adjusted to provide quality data.

Other areas used to help the users understand and know the data in the data lakehouse include:

- **Monitoring and alerts.** Refers to assessing, measuring, and managing data in the data lakehouse for accuracy, consistency, and reliability to detect data quality issues before the issue impacts an organization's business operations and customers. Data quality monitoring uses rules and criteria established by the users, and continuously monitors and checks the data. This can be completed through data profiling or data quality monitoring tools to identify any deficiencies or anomalies in the data. Alerts are provided when an issue is identified so this can be resolved before the user begins to use this data. Not all data is equal and carries the same need to be accurate, so it is important to identify the Critical Data Elements (CDEs) in the data lakehouse so these data fields can be evaluated and managed as priority data fields.

- **Subject domain considerations.** Refers to data issues specific to a subject domain area, including Sales, Inventory, Finance, Accounting, Marketing, Claims, Policies, Customers, and Products. Each subject domain may have data fields that are more critical to their decision making, and these data fields need to be evaluated and monitored more closely than other data fields.

- **Data values.** Refers to the data values or ranges of data values that should be populated in the data field. If the data values are not within these valid values, the data may cause faulty or inaccurate analysis. It is critical the users know and understand these issues in data to know the validity of each data field they are using for their analysis. Data profiling can be used to determine the valid values to help when identifying data issues or anomalies.

Index

PII. See Personally Identifiable
Information
preprocessing, 45, 46, 52, 55
privacy, 31, 80, 83, 84, 85, 89,
103, 154
probability of access, 61, 132,
133, 134, 135, 137, 141
Protected Health Information,
154, 155
protection, 83, 85
rate of growth of the data
lakehouse, 12
raw data, 7, 8, 10, 17, 58
relational, 111
relationships, 19, 111, 112, 114,
147, 148
relevance, 87, 88, 91, 95, 159
replication, 81
roadmap, 102, 143
Sarbanes-Oxley Act, 155
Savitzky-Golay, 54
security, 77, 83, 104, 118, 121,
129, 130, 154
smoothing, 45, 46, 53, 54, 55
SMS, 74
snowflake, 111, 113
Social Security Number, 19, 90,
154

SOX. See Sarbanes-Oxley Act
spreadsheet, 32
standard deviation, 49, 50, 51,
52
standardization, 47, 49, 50, 51,
70, 76, 119
star schema, 111
strategy, 92, 100, 102, 114, 116
structured environment, 13, 14,
145
taxonomy, 34, 35, 36, 146
technician, 6
textual, 5, 10, 11, 28, 33, 38, 39,
41, 64, 70, 71, 72, 76, 144, 145,
146, 148
threshold, 58
timeboxing, 59
transformation, 10, 24, 25, 46,
51, 75, 77, 78, 80, 81, 104, 106,
119
transformations, 16, 24
upsampling, 55
views, 88, 89, 113
visualization, 45, 104, 119
Zoom, 31
Z-score scaling, 49